CSR, Sustainability, Ethics & Governance

Series Editors

Samuel O. Idowu, London Metropolitan University, Calcutta House
London, UK

René Schmidpeter, Cologne Business School
Cologne, Germany

In recent years the discussion concerning the relation between business and society has made immense strides. This has in turn led to a broad academic and practical discussion on innovative management concepts, such as Corporate Social Responsibility, Corporate Governance and Sustainability Management. This series offers a comprehensive overview of the latest theoretical and empirical research and provides sound concepts for sustainable business strategies. In order to do so, it combines the insights of leading researchers and thinkers in the fields of management theory and the social sciences – and from all over the world, thus contributing to the interdisciplinary and intercultural discussion on the role of business in society. The underlying intention of this series is to help solve the world's most challenging problems by developing new management concepts that create value for business and society alike. In order to support those managers, researchers and students who are pursuing sustainable business approaches for our common future, the series offers them access to cutting-edge management approaches.

CSR, Sustainability, Ethics & Governance is accepted by the Norwegian Register for Scientific Journals, Series and Publishers, maintained and operated by the Norwegian Social Science Data Services (NSD)

Zamumtima Chijere

Nonprofit Social Enterprises

Lessons from Africa

Springer

Zamumtima Chijere
RiseMalawi Ministries
Lilongwe, Malawi

ISSN 2196-7075 ISSN 2196-7083 (electronic)
CSR, Sustainability, Ethics & Governance
ISBN 978-3-031-60233-7 ISBN 978-3-031-60234-4 (eBook)
https://doi.org/10.1007/978-3-031-60234-4

This Springer imprint is published by the registered company Springer Nature Switzerland AG
The registered company address is: Gewerbestrasse 11, 6330 Cham, Switzerland

To my amazing wife Dorothy whose care and emotional support has made it possible for me to finish this project.
and
To my son Ethan and my daughter Larissa.

Preface

The focus of this book is on the social enterprises that are operated by nonprofit organizations. It should be noted that not all nonprofit organizations engage in social enterprising or social entrepreneurship. In this book, nonprofit organizations engaged in revenue-generating ventures are regarded as social enterprising nonprofit organizations. I refer to these nonprofit organizations that engage in businesses that generate funds for the organizations to reinvest in their social obligation work Social Enterprising Nonprofit Organizations (SENOs).

It is important to note that social enterprise projects are activities carried out by individuals or groups of people working together for the good of others in society and not just for profit. My concern here focuses on nonprofit organizations that engage in business as a means to raise funds to achieve the organization's social mission. Social enterprises in nonprofit organizations thus engage in businesses that focus on fulfilling social causes with the profits that the enterprise makes. The social mission of social enterprises pertains to bringing about social transformation to a community. This social transformation is also known as a social cause by scholars and practitioners (Ko & Liu, 2020; Turpin & Shier, 2023; Dart, 2004; Drayton, 2011).

These organizations focus beyond surviving, they strive to flourish as well. In Aristotelian philosophy, flourishing is discussed in two dimensions. The first is eudaimonic well-being, which is associated with a sense of purpose or meaning in life. It conceptualizes well-being in the cultivation of personal strengths and contribution to the greater good while acting in accordance with inner values in the realization of one's true potential (Aristotle, 2000; Waterman, 1993). Then there is hedonic well-being, which often focuses on the degree of the experience of pleasure. It equates well-being with pleasure and happiness (Ryan & Deci, 2001). These attributes of flourishing pertain to individuals' well-being. Though flourishing is mostly discussed at individual level, there have been recent approach to understand it at organizational level.

In this book, you will embark on a journey through the heart and soul of the nonprofit social enterprise sector. You will encounter the stories of innovation, resilience, leadership, and unwavering dedication toward the greater good. These stories are not just about organizations; they are about people who have chosen to channel their passion and expertise into building social ventures that tackle some of the pressing issues facing our nations.

Nonprofit social enterprises present a unique fusion of business expertise and social conscience. They are not content to merely identify problems; they are driven to find sustainable solutions. They reject the notion that financial success and social impact are mutually exclusive. Instead, they operate in the fertile intercession where business and benevolence meet, proving that the pursuit of profit can be harnessed to fuel meaningful social change.

My first and only career has been in the nonprofit sector. Over the years, I have been deeply motivated to understand the nonprofit world, especially in developing countries. I am keen to understand the dynamics of flourishing that is occurring in social enterprising nonprofit organizations in many ways. It touches the heart of what I am and what I do in my daily life. Thus, it has long been my desire to discover emerging approaches to running social enterprising nonprofits both in Africa and across the world. Additionally, my professional career has been leaning toward nonprofit governance and leadership, especially in the area of managing organizational performance. I founded a social enterprising nonprofit organization. This unique position as an indigenous nonprofit founder and leader gives me a deep desire to understand nonprofits and social enterprises in developing countries like Malawi.

Another reason for studying social enterprises emerged after I saw the struggle that many nonprofit organizations encounter, especially in raising funds for their operations. I have come to realize through experience in working in Malawi with different organizations, both indigenous and international, that many nonprofit organizations struggle to sustain themselves. This has driven me to seek a deeper understanding of nonprofit operations, especially their social enterprising activities. This book provides a guiding model on how to run flourishing enterprises.

As you turn these pages, you will discover that nonprofit social enterprises are not a passing trend, but a growing force that is reshaping the way we think about success, resilience, and flourishing of social enterprises. I invite you to embark on a journey to understand flourishing in nonprofit social enterprises. Whether you are a seasoned nonprofit leader, an upcoming social entrepreneur, or simply someone curious about the flourishing and management of nonprofit social enterprises, this book has something to offer you. Let the stories in these pages not only be a source of operating flourishing entities whether for-profit or nonprofit not just for financial success but also for the betterment of humanity. It is my belief that the promise, the mission, and the hope of nonprofit social enterprises are worth to be embarked upon by many scholars.

Finally, this book is a guide for those who aspire to create their own nonprofit social enterprises. It will help them to understand what it means to flourish. It will provide invaluable insight, practical advice, and inspiration from those who have gone before us. This book is a roadmap for navigating the challenges, seizing opportunities, and ultimately making a lasting difference in the communities.

Lilongwe, Malawi

Zamumtima Chijere

Acknowledgments

First, I want to thank God almighty for making this project possible.

I wish to thank Dorothy, my wife, for the moral support she gave me during my studies. She has been a wonderful companion and friend. I have been away from home on numerous occasions, but she has been understanding all the way. Her support has been instrumental in the success of this study.

Dr. Mike Mtika for his guidance throughout this process has been influential in the quality of this work. He pushed me into a deeper thinking process in this final study. I also want to thank Dr. Heewon Chang and Dr. David Bronkema for their guidance and important counsel in this field of study. They pushed me to better academic writing and making this work more practical. I owe them an enormous debt of gratitude for their time, expertise, and support.

Ms. Tinashe Saka, my friend and co-worker who has been a great partner for the past 20 years. I appreciate her for having taken up my workload during the numerous times I have been focusing on this project.

I would also like to thank Mr. Chimwemwe Chijere, my young brother. I also recognize the support from Dr. Paul Kamlongera, Mr. Gibozi Mphanzi, Mr. Malason Kachipanda, Ms. Dorothy Kamoto, Mr. Willie Mpasuka, and Mr. Fascio Chijere. You come to my aid on many occasions in editing when I needed a second set of eyes to my work.

To Jeffie Abbot. To Martin and Mary Bond. To Dr. Linda Stines. Their moral and financial support have been instrumental during my years of research and writing this book. They have been a wonderful support to my work in Malawi.

Finally, I owe huge debt and gratitude to Dr. Bruce Main. He has been a great mentor to me.

Contents

Chapter 1
An Overview on Social Enterprises and Nonprofit Organizations

The practice of social enterprising has become a critical practice in community development for many nonprofit organizations over the past two decades. Scholars such as Hung et al. and Turpin and Shier (2023) have highlighted the emerging importance of social enterprises to the survival and success of nonprofit organizations, especially in implementing social change in communities. As a result of a combination of funding cuts to social programs from various donors and a change in meeting their social transformation goals, many nonprofit organizations have resorted to social enterprising as an organizational survival tactic. Instead of doing their work in the traditional or conventional way—that is, raising funds from donors to implement planned projects—many nonprofit organizations now engage in social enterprising or business activities through which they generate funds and invest these funds into their community development activities (Pizarro et al., 2022). In this regard, nonprofits are seizing upon social enterprising as a way to fill the gap left by donor cutbacks. Social enterprises help nonprofit organizations to engage in commercial activities to fill this funding cutback (Svensson et al., 2020; Kerlin, 2006). According to Kerlin and others, the idea is to move into more market-driven strategies in order to raise needed funds for social projects.

In the past three decades, nonprofit organizations in developing countries, especially indigenous ones, have increasingly engaged in social enterprising. López-Arceiz et al. (2023) explain that this evolution toward the social enterprise model evidenced by the generation of income is the result of the interaction between socio-political developments and organizational change. The goal of these organizations has been to sustainably continue their operations. In other words, their goal has been to flourish; this is the goal of any organization (Borji, 2020; Coupet & Berrett (2019); Ryan & Deci, 2001).

This chapter discusses the emergence of social enterprising and the different approaches of social enterprises, the philology of flourishing, and the success and performance factors in social enterprising nonprofit organizations. I will first provide introductory background on the emergence of social enterprises and the

Z. Chijere, *Nonprofit Social Enterprises*, CSR, Sustainability, Ethics & Governance, https://doi.org/10.1007/978-3-031-60234-4_1

philosophy of flourishing at both the individual and organizational levels. I will thereafter shed light on the origins and operations of nonprofit organizations before venturing into social enterprising as an emerging area within development studies and practice.

1.1 An Overview on Social Enterprises and Nonprofit Organizations

Social entrepreneurs, as the study has intimated in the previous chapter, undertake social enterprising. A "social entrepreneur" is an ambitious person who seeks social change, characteristically through earned income strategies (López-Arceiz et al., 2023; Brown, 2003). Social entrepreneurs aim at creating a "social economy" for a community through their innovative solutions to social issues and problems. The objectives of a social economy include the creation of employment, stable jobs, access to work for disadvantaged groups, the provision of services, and training and personal development opportunities (Brown, 2003; Doherty et al., 2014). In this regard, some social entrepreneurs focus on enterprising strategies that create a revenue base with the aim of supporting the social obligation of transforming a community. Mikołajczak (2020) explain that social enterprises are therefore an expression of the possibility of different institutional logics coexisting as part of the same organization.

A growing number of nonprofit organizations is embracing and pursuing earned income strategies for their operation and as a survival strategy. In many cases, this is a means to reduce their dependence on donations and grants. Historically, nonprofit organizations have been dependent on donations from international donors, the state, and other agencies for the implementation of their programs (López-Arceiz et al., 2023; Suykens et al. 2021; Battilana et al., 2017). Through nonprofit social enterprising, an organization is proactive in generating revenue to be invested in community development ventures.

Social enterprises basically take three forms. These are sustainable enterprises, blended value organizations, and socially responsible companies (Rask et al., 2020). A detailed discussion of differences on these three forms is beyond my interest here. In regard to nonprofit organizations, suffice to say that the social enterprising approach reduces donor control over an organization's activities because earned income, unlike donations, is generally unencumbered by donor-imposed restrictions on its use (Haeffele & Storr, 2019; Hopp & Stephan, 2012). This basically means that a nonprofit organization can generate profits at the institutional level, in which it is free to use in meeting its social obligations. To maintain nonprofit status, revenues generated must return to the organization's work. These organizations ought to have the "the dominant value of ultraism combined with dominant means for profit" (Rask et al., 2020, p. 2). Others (e.g., Sabeti et al., 2014) refer to such organizations as Fourth Sector Organizations, an emerging sector of the economy that combines market-based approaches in the private sector with the social and environmental aims of the nonprofit and public sectors. Battilana et al. (2017) contended that these organizations have two primary attributes of social purpose and business method. It should be noted that the emerging social enterprising sector is becoming dominant and that in the near future, it will reshape the future of world economies (Sabeti et al., 2014).

Whether practiced by nonprofit or for-profit organizations, as focused on here, social enterprising provides leaders with an institutional framework for establishing an independent means of financing programs directed at addressing social issues and problems. It is argued that the integration of business tools and practices with nonprofit work builds capacity that can improve performance and increase organizations' ability to effect lasting change (Crace et al., 2023; Suykens et al., 2021; Alter, 2000). The goal is to have self-sufficient organizations through earned income rather than donations. However, social enterprising organization leaders are obliged to do more than merely refraining from diverting the entity's surplus to themselves; they have an affirmative duty to advance the organization's mission.

1.2 The History and Emergence of Nonprofit Organizations

Solving social problems in developing countries has historically been the responsibility of governments and philanthropic institutions. However, because of the difficulties governments face worldwide in meeting the needs of citizens, nonprofit organizations arose to help the governments' social responsibility (Williamson et al., 2011). Nonprofit organizations in developing countries have intervened in times when governments increasingly struggled to provide timely and effective interventions to mounting crises.

Of note, organizations are classified into three major sectors: public, private, and third sector (Crace et al., 2023; Bruni-Bossio & Willness, 2016). Public organizations are government-sponsored. Private organizations are owned by individuals or institutions and are mostly profit-oriented. Generally, the private sector is defined as a business sector. The third sector is generally referred to as the nonprofit sector or the nongovernmental sector. There is an accepted degree of substitution of the term nongovernmental organizations across scholarship internationally. The terms include nonprofit, third sector organizations, civil society organizations, and not-for-profits (Bukhini et al., 2014). Each country uses one of these terms to refer to organizations that provide services that the private sectors do not or services that complement what the government is doing.

The proliferation of nonprofit organizations in developing as well as developed countries has triggered an "associational revolution" (Clarke, 1998). This "associational revolution" has brought about nonprofit professional organizations with a distinctive legal character and is concerned with public welfare goals. Shivji (2007), in *Silences in NGO Discourse: The Role and Future of NGOs in Africa*, posited that the rise in prominence of nonprofit organizations' aims is a product of ideological, economic, and political discourse. Nonprofit organizations take the approach of philanthropic foundations, church development agencies, academic institutions, and other organizations that focus on issues such as human rights, gender, health, agricultural development, social welfare, the environment, and indigenous peoples. These organizations are primarily characterized by humanitarian or cooperative goals rather than commercial objectives. Toward this end, they pursue activities to relieve suffering, promote the interests of the poor, protect the environment, provide basic social services, or undertake community development (Audretsch et al., 2020a; Ahmed, 2003).

The rise of nonprofit organizations in developing countries has proliferated due to several significant factors. First, governments in developed countries channel significant amounts of aid and money to developing countries through these organizations. Second, multilateral and bilateral donors are following the same trend of channeling aid through nonprofit organizations (Salmon, 2008). Salmon observed that in a climate of dissatisfaction with the governments of developing countries and under pressure from member states, multilateral donors and their bilateral partners have channeled increasing amounts of funding through nonprofit organizations rather than through the recipient governments. Third, the dictatorial governments in many developing countries that were hostile to nonprofit organizations were forced by economic recession in the 1980s to concede greater recognition and involve the organizations in socioeconomic programs. In many developing countries, large-scale social movements rose after the fall of dictatorial movements. Multiparty democracy gave rise to freedom, of which the freedom to form associations was one. Management of social enterprising nonprofit organizations is a critical factor in their success or demise (Crace et al., 2023). The way they are managed can lead to their flourishing or death.

1.3 The Major Discourses on Social Enterprises

Management of nonprofit organizations and their social enterprising ventures occur within major discourses that have guided enterprising processes. A review of its history and emergence clearly reveals the discourses that prompted the evolution and operations of social enterprising. There are three major discourses in the nature and understanding of social enterprising.

The first discourse is linked to the form or type of the nonprofit organizations venturing into business activities for social transformation. Jean-Baptiste Say (1767–1832), a French economist, perceived social enterprising within the context of a social entrepreneur who undertakes an idea and shifts perspectives in a way that alters how things are done in society. This has led to numerous studies (e.g., Shier et al., 2019; Haeffele & Storr, 2019; Luke & Chu, 2013) describing how the discipline has unfolded over a period of time. Social enterprising is a practice that started to gain prominence during the last half of the nineteenth century in the broad context of civil society and international development. Say suggested the existence of some similarity between a social entrepreneur and a traditional entrepreneur. He recognized that entrepreneurs use economic resources in the society to reach higher productivity and greater yield, and what one needs to do is to just add the word social to entrepreneur. De Vries (1988) pointed out that Hegel, although not explicitly talking about social entrepreneurs, referred to them as world-class individuals, heroic men and women with insight into what was needed for the current time. They challenged the status quo through their disruptive, seemingly dysfunctional, approaches to innovate, change, and deliver greater social impact. Social entrepreneurs are thus socially enterprising.

The second discourse on social enterprising addresses the rise of credit unions. Credit unions are regarded as community- or national-based financial institutions that provide savings and loan facilities to members of a community (Mikołajczak, 2020; Ko & Liu, 2020; Kelly, 2009; World Bank, 2012). The goal is to give individuals an opportunity to access funds that will help in funding their entrepreneurial ideas. As long as these entrepreneurial ideas push one to engage in socially beneficial business ventures, the people are engaging in social enterprising.

The last discourse on social enterprising revolves around business imperatives, particularly when a highly profitable firm takes a stand to engage in fully fledged external corporate social responsibility in response to unmet social needs. Some scholars (e.g., Ko & Liu, 2020; Turpin & Shier, 2023; Hopp & Stephan, 2012) believed this would be a better way to go in social enterprising as opposed to relying on donors and the state for revenue. Others call them "hybrid social ventures" (Hung & Wang, 2021; Battilana et al., 2017; Kelly, 2009) since they operate simultaneously as two entities with two different missions. Others prefer to call them businesses companies with a conscience (Heerad Sabeti et al., 2014), or "for profit with a nonprofit soul" (Lang, 2015), or "fair trade" (Harvey, 2017; Mayo, 2017). In this regard, scholars have asserted that for-profit businesses also focus on social missions by dedicating some of their work to addressing social ills. Profit is the primary goal, but they make sure that they also pursue the social goals of the organization. They aim at achieving both financial and social return on investment. Turpin and Shier (2023) concurred with this by illustrating how a highly profitable firm may participate in meeting social needs through various stances in corporate social responsibility. This thought is supported by Pizarro et al. (2022) and Brolis and Nyssens (2019) understanding of social enterprising, which points out that social enterprising organizations are private sector businesses geared toward social regeneration rather than simply the generation of profits.

1.4 Governance and Management of Nonprofit Organizations

Governance is derived from Latin and Greek which originally meant guidance, control, and manipulation. It refers to a set of actors that exert power and authority to maintain order to meet the needs of an organization (Colebatch, 2017; Keping, 2018). This is done through the enactment of policies and decisions concerning the operation of the organization. On the other hand, management involves establishing systems and processes that ensure the overall direction, effectiveness, supervision, and accountability of an organization (Ko & Liu, 2020; Brolis & Nyssens, 2019). Governance and management play a pivotal role in ensuring the success of organizations. Most organizations fall or rise based on their governance and management systems. A well-designed board of trustees, carefully selected staff, and dedicated board members help an organization meet its mission and goals. This means that governance encompasses several things within the organization system. Shier et al. (2019) pointed out that governance mechanisms include governing boards, monitoring systems, and signaling systems like reporting or codes of conduct. He bemoaned the fact that many leaders in social enterprising organizations are reluctant to create governance structures that will control the operations of the institution. The importance of these structures lies in overseeing compliance with policies and regulations. These structures also protect the organizations' missions while meeting stakeholders' demands. However, all of this also depends at what stage of evolution the nonprofit finds itself. Most nonprofits start out small, with boards that include founders, and then evolve into a more structured model.

Nonprofit organizations are controlled by their board of trustees, which does not personally profit from their association and decision. Most organizations have one-tier board management, while others have two-tier boards, comprising the board of trustees and the executive board. Cornforth and Brown (2013) remarked that the board's main responsibility is governance of the organization. The board of trustees is generally the controller of an organization's activities and is assigned both the legal and fiduciary responsibility (Mikołajczak, 2020). It makes policies, makes decisions in regard to the operation of the organization, and is accountable for those policies and decisions. The boards of nonprofit organizations, for example, provide strategic support and expertise on operations. They also provide access to networks that will bring resources and technical support to the operation of the organization. Above all, they signal credibility to external stakeholders like investors, customers, and contractors. An organization's management team is responsible to the board for carrying out what the board has stipulated as the organization's mission, policies, and operational procedures that should be followed. Management is responsible to the board for the use of resources (human, financial, physical, and others) in fulfilling the policies and decisions of the board. It is noted that job satisfaction in an organization is affected by the management approaches of the organization. In this regard, management of the organizations will facilitate an organizational climate that motivates or demotivates the employees (Kurtessis et al., 2017).

1.5 Chapter Conclusion

The shrinking of resources for the nonprofit organization has led the nonprofit organization sector to find other means of raising the most needed funds as they meet the social obligation of the organization. The nonprofit organizations have found social enterprising as a way of supplementing their resources.

Chapter 2
The Emergence and Operation of Social Enterprising Nonprofit Organizations

In recent years, a significant number of social enterprising nonprofit organizations have arisen around the globe, representing ever-growing interest in the practice (López-Arceiz et al., 2023; Chell, 2010; Dees & Anderson, 2003; Nicholls, 2010). This growth has been necessitated by several pull-push factors that are affecting the global economy, especially in regard to the social economy and the development of communities. The pull-push factors are elements that drive away or pull out certain ways and push in new innovative ways of doing things. In geography, the term is used to describe why people migrate from one area to another.

Social enterprising has received increasing attention from both academics and practitioners both in the nonprofit and private sector. Social enterprises in nonprofit organizations are revenue-generating ventures, founded for purposes of supporting or creating economic opportunities while simultaneously operating social mission activities (activities addressing social issues and problems) of a nonprofit organization (López-Arceiz et al., 2023; Ko & Liu, 2020). In nonprofit organizations, social enterprises are business ventures that aim at supporting the operations of nonprofit organization activities. In most cases, they have governing structures and stipulations different from those of purely nonprofit entities. One of the major goals of nonprofit social enterprises is to raise revenue for nonprofit organizations. Cadwell thus defined a social enterprise as "a cause-driven business, whose primary reason for existing is to improve social objectives and serve the common good" (p. 8).

2.1 Social Entrepreneurship vs. Social Enterprising

Social enterprising for nonprofit organizations is closely linked to the practice of social entrepreneurship. In most instances, the concept of social enterprise is taken as a branch of social entrepreneurship. The terms "social entrepreneurship" and

Z. Chijere, *Nonprofit Social Enterprises*, CSR, Sustainability, Ethics & Governance, https://doi.org/10.1007/978-3-031-60234-4_2

"social entrepreneurs" first appeared in Bowen's 1953 book, *Social Responsibilities of the Businessman*. Bowen saw the need for innovation in meeting the bottom line in social organizations. Bowen promoted the idea of running businesses that reinvested the money they made back into the local community. From the early 1980s to 1990s, scholars like Leadbeater (2006) and Laszlo promoted the concept of social entrepreneurship in their various writings. Leadebeater's work focused on the behavior of social entrepreneurs as they focused on bringing about social change. Drayton, the founder of Ashoka, who has written extensively on social entrepreneurship as a practice, explains that there is solid evidence that social entrepreneurs have helped in addressing many social issues and problems, focusing on how entrepreneurs act and do their work to have some social impact (Drayton, 2019).

Many scholars believe that the concept of social entrepreneurship is poorly defined, which results in fuzzy boundaries in research and practice (Barman, 2008; Carman & Nesbit, 2013; Yusuf & Sloan, 2015). Scholars associate entrepreneurship with opportunity, innovation, and risk. For this study, I draw on Schumpeter's work and define entrepreneurship as a process of creation or identification and exploitation of opportunities through creative destruction (Littlewood & Holt, 2015; Schumpeter, 1934). In this respect, social entrepreneurship involves "the recognition, evaluation, and exploitation of opportunities which result in social value" (Salamzadeh et al., 2012, p. 521). This creation of social value happens by deconstructing old understandings of social problems and bringing in more innovative solutions.

A social enterprise thus has a profit goal with the objective of the profit being invested in a social mission. In principle, the hallmark of a social enterprise is its ability to combine social interests with business practices to effect social change (Turpin & Shier, 2023; Anderson, 2015; Luke & Chu, 2013). The goal of running such businesses is to create social value in the community (Hung & Wang, 2021; Carman & Nesbit, 2013; Littlewood, 2018). Thus, an individual or organization running a social enterprise must be entrepreneurial. These social enterprising nonprofit organizations (SENOs) are socially entrepreneurial in that they creatively use social enterprising as a fundraising tool to sustain the organizations' social mission.

2.1.1 Factors That Led to the Emergence of SENOs

Funding cuts for social programs have forced many nonprofit organizations to develop income-generating strategies to finance programs directed at addressing social issues and problems. Studies (e.g., Burde et al., 2017; Chirwa, 2016) have shown that public funding available to nonprofit organizations has drastically declined in the past decade. Tough world economic conditions have seen nonprofits struggling to raise the much-needed revenue in order to operate effectively. This has induced the nonprofit sector to search for market-based interventions to increase sustainability, and that in turn has led nonprofit organizations to explore social enterprising. Hung et al. (2019) stated that the majority of nonprofit organizations are transforming their operational models from donor dependence to self-funding.

This funding cut is one of the major motivators for organizations to venture into more innovative ways of raising funds. As a result, according to Biddulph (2018), the adoption of pro-business behavior and techniques to supplement funding to later lead to the fulfillment of provision for the community has become necessary. As Shier et al. (2019) and Suykens et al. (2021) explained, the donor or state, "dependency syndrome" and disempowerment effects associated with donor/state- and nonprofit-subsidized programs have led to the realization that the organization's mission can never be fulfilled if states and other donors are the only source of funds. Thus, nonprofit organizations need to find other avenues for expanding their revenue base. Social enterprising has become the best approach whereby nonprofits are using business strategies to generate more income. This has become an urgent matter, as social problems in developing economies are enormous and donations to traditional nonprofit organizations are drying up.

Secondly, the current "pro-business zeitgeist" has made social enterprising more fashionable (Battilana et al. 2017; Dees et al., 1998; Helmsing, 2015). This factor attracts nonprofit organizations to venture into social enterprising, which is the spirit driving the current generation of social entrepreneurs (Turpin and Shier, 2023). It has become the most popular approach to meeting the social needs of a community through business ventures. Governments across the developing world have abandoned traditional public administration for contemporary new public management, where cost recovery on all government services has become the norm.

In more general terms, the complexity of current development problems, which need different kinds of actors and actor configurations to address them, has attracted the individuals with a business mindset to address social problems (Becchetti & Borzaga, 2010; Suykens et al., 2021). For instance, the Government of Malawi has established several social cash transfer programs whereby money is granted to poor and labor-constrained households as a means of creating revenue within a community, which in turn helps in the community's development. This approach is also being adopted by several other organizations and for-profit enterprises. Individuals are finding social enterprising, unlike the traditional way of doing community work, to be an effective means of developing communities. Kieng and Quack (2012) pointed out that in Southern Africa in particular, citizens are highly dependent on government resources despite the governments' growing inability to meet citizens' social needs. This context calls for individuals with a social business mindset to fill the gap left by the state. Social enterprising then marries the dichotomy of nonprofit and for-profit entities to create both social and economic value within a new type of institution. However, the success of these new institutions is not yet clear.

Thirdly, the complexity of social problems calls for complex approaches to solving them. As discussed earlier, social enterprising creates a social economy that provides the community with different opportunities to alleviate their suffering. As a pull-push factor, social enterprising provides options to developing communities for sustaining their development. The Social Enterprise UK report of 2016 revealed that by selling goods and services on the open market, social enterprising nonprofits use profits to improve people's lives and support communities. This is a new and creative intervention in helping to solve social problems. As opposed to giving the profit back to the shareholders for their own personal use, revenue generated through social enterprising is used in accordance with its social mission, leading to the making of a positive difference in the world by way of reinvesting the profits made in the open market into goods that benefits the broader society (Audretsch et al., 2020b; Manders et al., 2020; Bradshaw, 2009).

Profits generated by social enterprising nonprofit organizations are sometimes misused, which leads to organizations failing to improve people's well-being. This is basically due to the fact that most such organizations have no clear operating procedures as social enterprises. This underscores the need for clear understanding of who holds the social enterprising organizations accountable to their mission. A major concern is that social enterprising in nonprofits, aimed at benefiting society by reinvesting funds raised through their business ventures, compromises the motivation to continue maximizing profits compared to traditional enterprises, whose profits and impact can easily be measured (López-Arceiz et al., 2023; Mikołajczak, 2020).

2.2 The Element of Management in Social Enterprises

Social enterprising nonprofit organizations introduce a new nonprofit model for creating sustainable value for people. It has become the avenue through which enterprising nonprofit organizations are raising funds to meet social responsibilities. This does not turn the involved nonprofit organizations into purely profit focused businesses; rather, business entrepreneurial skills and attitudes are simply seen as necessities for survival. This means that organizations tend to adopt the concept of "commercialization" in order to successfully run nonprofit organizations (Bradshaw, 2009). However, the assumption that each social enterprising venture can generate profit should be called into question based on whether each one of them can develop the capability necessary to achieve competitive advantage as a business. Nonetheless, a unique approach would necessitate the nonprofit organization becoming enterprising. Porter (2008) wrote extensively on the need of a profit-making firm to make unique moves in the market in order to be effective. Porter's Five Forces Framework is one of the widely used tools for analyzing competition of a business. In Porter's model, the five forces that shape industry competition are competitive rivalry, bargaining power of suppliers, bargaining power of customers, threat of new entrants, and threat of substitute products or services. The framework helps in determining attractiveness or lack thereof in an industry in terms of profitability. An organization can thus strategically position itself in the industry into which it ventures. This puts social enterprises into a double bind: they rely on self-funding involving penetrating markets but do so to fulfill their social missions to their clients (Luke & Chu, 2013).

The commercial nature of social enterprising organizations raises the question of their capability to develop core competencies required for any revenue-generating firm to attain competitive advantage. This demands that an organization attends to both business and social mission orientations. Literature on management emphasizes that if a firm is to sustain its operations or achieve a competitive advantage, it must possess competencies in bringing enough resources for the enterprising organization operating with business motives for the purpose of generating profits and should also possess the required business competencies. This is critical, since the business approach is mostly different from that of nonprofit management systems.

Social enterprising organizations do not engage in shared capital to the benefit of shareholders. As a result, neither dividends nor financial returns are the focus of social enterprising operations. Instead, social enterprising organizations generate revenue not to profit the owners of social enterprising organizations, but for addressing social issues and problems. Of course, there have been some transformations in the business world where the role of the business has expanded to doing social good (Alfakhri, 2018; Carroll, 2015). All the same, social enterprising organizations tend to use language similar to that for-profit organizations such as market, opportunity, competitiveness, and other related business terminology to thrive and survive. The management of the social enterprising process could actually be different. Social enterprising organizations basically utilize "the art of simultaneously pursuing both a financial and a social return on the investment" (Sabiti et al., 2014). This is what others (Hopp & Stephan, 2012) term as the double bottom line in the management of these organizations. This means that a social enterprise has both a social responsibility and simultaneously the business perspective to make profits. The organizations cannot survive and grow and meet their social aims unless they make a profit. Nicholls (2010) explained that entrepreneurs in social enterprising organizations work by employing nonprofit, for-profit, and hybrid organizational forms to deliver social value. The entrepreneurs seek to use for-profit approaches to generate income for social ventures. Brolis and Nyssens (2019) concurred with Nichols, explaining that social enterprising could be termed civic innovation—that is, entities that are aimed at generating revenue to support social visions. Nevertheless, the greater purpose of social enterprising is to benefit the public rather than the accumulation of profit for owners (Mikołajczak, 2020; Arasti et al., 2014). However, the dual function of social enterprising continues to make social enterprising complex. For instance, the balancing of social and business objectives is completely contrary to the principles of nonprofit management, especially in developing countries. The desire to maximize profit-making and the yearning to see returns are completely at odds with the elements of nonprofit governance and regulations in many developing countries.

The other important element in managing social enterprises is the issue of culture. Nonprofit and for-profit organizations operate in different dimensions of culture. The business sector focuses on profit margins as the major measure of performance, which is different from the nonprofit sector. Pizarro et al. (2022), Suykens et al. (2021), and Arasti et al. (2014) contended that a nonprofit organization getting into social enterprising inadequately considers issues that deal with managing culture. The once-charitable entity is founded on a culture that, if not changed, cannot support the drive toward entrepreneurial behavior. The operations of many nonprofit organizations do not provide a platform that drives individuals to productivity, unlike the private sector. Nonetheless, both theoretical and empirical literature on social enterprising provides inadequate guidelines on issues of cultural transformation.

2.3 Theories on the Rise of Social Enterprising

There are four theories regarding the rise of social enterprising organizations. The first is the neoliberal theory, as expounded by Dey (2006). The view here is that states are unable to deliver welfare services and that there are no trade-offs between social and economic goals in capitalist economies (Blackburn & Ram, 2006). This view has several other names, but all basically refer to the same approach. For instance, Eriksen called it a "state failure theory," which focuses on the inability of states to meet the citizenry's needs. Thus, it is argued that social enterprising organizations arise to fill the gap left by the state to meet the social needs of the citizens.

The second is what scholars call the "third way" or communitarian theory (Grenier & Guberman, 2009). This theory argues that social enterprising emerged to benefit the community; profit distribution to external investors should thus be limited at all costs (Defourny & Nyssens, 2006). This applies to for-profit firms that view social enterprising as a social obligation. This theory drives for-profit businesses operating in the social welfare field to deliberately create avenues to meet the needs of the suffering masses (Kanter & Purrington, 1998). Others take this theory as the belief that for-profit enterprises display some social conscience in meeting communities' social needs (Harding, 2010). In this regard, private sector organizations deliberately create strategies to meet the societal needs that are basically addressed by nonprofit organizations.

The third is the market failure theory, which espouses the view that inequitable distribution of goods in free markets is creating more social problems among the poor (Mikołajczak, 2020). Social enterprising thus creates profit that will help the disadvantaged with the goal of enabling the disadvantaged to access resources to meet their needs. This is also referred to as the social economy approach by some scholars (e.g., Osberg & Martin, 2015). It calls for a more radical tradition that sees capitalism itself as the problem. Thus, social enterprising helps to address common economic, social, and cultural needs through jointly owned and democratically controlled enterprises. Social enterprising agents are expected to use structures, business models, and tools to achieve their desired end in an existing equilibrium (Hung et al., 2019).

Finally, the resource dependency theory expounded by Dees (1998) proposes that nonprofit organizations' increased reliance on earned income is associated with cutbacks in philanthropic giving. The state does not have the capacity to deliver welfare services (Teasdale, 2010). The theory contends that decreased government attention to welfare demands is pushing social enterprising organizations to create sources of income. Whatever the school of thought, social enterprises have a well-defined operational approach.

Regardless of the reasons for the rise of social enterprising, it is particularly becoming very important in nonprofit organizations. In the African context, the social enterprising nonprofit organizations sector has not yet stabilized and could still be in the cognitive or consolidation stage of development. Lack of stability could mean lack of operational capacity, which includes inadequate skills or no effective network that can allow the sector to interact productively with governments, foreign NGOs, and other institutions. It is not clear whether thousands of social enterprises in Africa have access to international funding like the large-scale organizations working at the international level. Nor does the literature say much about the potential of African nonprofit organizations (NPOs) to generate sustainable resources internally. The theoretical framework on the understanding of social enterprising particularly in a developing country remains a matter for further research.

2.4 Chapter Conclusion

In this chapter, we have seen that there are many factors that led to the rise of social enterprising. These factors are regarded as elements that force the institutions into creative ways of engaging in enterprising activities. These pull-push factors include economic crises, the complexity of social problems, the inability of some governments to meet the social needs of their constituencies, the social enterprise mentality becoming more fashionable, a widening gap between rich and poor in many developed countries, and—for many—a less than appealing, scandal-ridden corporate world, among many others (Bornstein et al., 2016). The practice and the concept of social enterprise has been studied extensively across the globe. However, the flourishing of social enterprising nonprofit organizations has received little attention over the years. There is a great need to understand what makes social enterprising nonprofit organizations flourish, especially in developing countries.

Chapter 3
The Organizational Flourishing

The concept of organizational flourishing incorporates two dimensions of happiness: feeling good and functioning well. Individuals "feel good" has the capability of helping the employees functioning psychologically and socially well. This in turn influences the "functioning well" of the organizations' outcomes with respect to flourishing. As highlighted earlier, flourishing individuals inform the flourishing of an organization. Therefore, organizations that aim to develop their workforce and provide an avenue for employee flourishing have more potential to flourish than those that do not provide flourishing avenues for their workforce.

3.1 The Classical Understanding of Flourishing

There is an unbreakable connection between individual and organizational flourishing. Flourishing individuals inform the flourishing of an institution, and vice versa. To flourish is of course the goal of any organization, just as it is the goal of any individual in his or her life. Flourishing for nonprofit organizations that operate social enterprises is not just about success (Diener et al., 2010; Keyes, 2002; McLellan & Steward, 2015; Seligman, 2011). Flourishing is to live a certain end of life, and this activity implies a rational principle, and the function of a good man is the good and noble performance of these, and if any action is well performed, it is performed in accord with the appropriate excellence: if this is the case, then happiness turns out to be an activity of the soul in accordance with virtue (Aristotle, trans. 1991). Flourishing is not necessarily achieving an end, but living well as individuals strive to achieve that end. For Aristotle, the goodness of character is a settled condition of the soul which wills or chooses the means relatively by ourselves, this means being determined by a rule or whatever we like to call that by which the wise man determines it (Aristotle, trans. 1991). This is what Aristotle terms virtue. Flourishing, according to Aristotle, is closely linked with virtuous life. Building on Aristotle,

Z. Chijere, *Nonprofit Social Enterprises*, CSR, Sustainability, Ethics & Governance, https://doi.org/10.1007/978-3-031-60234-4_3

Keyes (2002, 2005) contended that the flourishing individual has a high level of emotional, social, and psychological well-being. Therefore, flourishing is not a state; it is an activity "going well." Aristotle observed that people have natural desires and capacities to know and understand the truth, pursue moral excellence, and instantiate their ideals in the world through action. Human achievements are animated by purpose and autonomy, and people should take pride in being excellent at what they do.

Aristotle advocates for a life of virtue as a means of achieving flourishing in life. He believed that life demands unity, since unity facilitates the protection of the rights of all citizens. For Aristotle, people must make different contributions in fulfilling different roles that will ensure self-sufficiency. Aristotle thought the notion of perfect beauty (*kalon*) becomes the center of any good person in the act of virtue. In his writings, especially the *Nicomachean Ethics*, Aristotle specifically mentions the life of gratification, the life of moneymaking, the life of action, and the philosophical life (the life of contemplation or study) as central to flourishing. He writes that the ultimate end is that which is desirable in itself and never for the sake of something else (Aristotle, trans. 1991).

Aristotle views human beings as rational animals that live in societies. He explains that human beings are not just rational, but also social; they thus become *interculturally competent* (in other words, they flourish) when they are able to live and learn from each other. Therefore, human beings are able to reach their end (flourish) through interaction.

In the *Nicomachean Ethics*, Aristotle says that *eudaimonia*, "doing and living well," is critical to flourishing (Aristotle, trans. 1991). The one who is flourishing, he asserted, is the one living "the good life." Aristotle gave a clear link between happiness or flourishing and integrity/ethics. This is what he later called the life of virtue. Aristotle believed that people flourish by living well and that they cannot live well if they lack the practical wisdom to engage in virtuous activities.

Aristotle distinguished two kinds of virtue. The first, called virtue of mind or intellect, pertains to the part of the soul that engages in reasoning. As explained by Gilkey (2008), intellectual virtue has two forms: one that relates to theoretical reasoning and the other to practical thinking. The second kind of virtue pertains to the part of the soul that cannot itself reason but is nonetheless capable of following reason (ethical virtue, virtue of character). I would contend that institutional investment in virtue would facilitate organizational flourishing. In this regard, organizations cannot achieve a flourishing state simply by enjoying the present pleasures of the moment. Instant gratification is what leads many institutions to fail to flourish. Since knowledge, according to Aristotle, is one of the central areas for the "good life," organizations become more virtuous and more able to flourish through education and habit of individuals. Knowledge investment should thus be part of the innate character of any institution. The same is highlighted by Scharmer and Käufer (2013) in their seminal work *Theory U or Leading from the Emerging Future*. Viewing flourishing from an organizational perspective, they contend that flourishing is closely linked with the emotional and social well-being of people and activities within an organization.

Aristotle also believed that knowledge can be obtained through interaction with physical objects. That is, the best way to lead one's life and to give it meaning is to discover what the supreme good is for man. The best way to look at things, according to Aristotle, is by looking at their ends. Aristotle thought that it is obvious that our proper functioning consists in reasoning and in acting in accord with reason. This is the heart of the doctrine of virtue, both moral and intellectual. Following this line of reasoning, we are led to the conclusion that the possession and exercise of moral and intellectual virtue are the essential elements of our living well, our flourishing. Happiness combines an element over which we have greater control (virtue) with elements over which we have less control (health, wealth, friends, etc.). Aristotle believed that the development of intellectual and moral virtue is the only backdrop against which such questions can be investigated fruitfully. Therefore, organizations that make a deliberate effort to train their people (a difficult and long task) are the ones that eventually attain flourishing.

3.2 Flourishing in the Modern World

As it was in classical times, human flourishing is regarded as a fundamental aspect of life in the modern era. Flourishing in this regard is described in part as the actualization of human potential, which is an essential element of a whole life (Seligman & Csikszentmihalyi, 2000). In modern times, flourishing is seen in the works of Alasdair MacIntyre, in the concept of positive psychology (PP) and in positive organization behavior (POB).

Alasdair MacIntyre posed the same questions raised by Aristotle but with an understanding of the modern individual. He asks about meaningful human life, which focuses on one's understanding of happiness in terms of human satisfaction. MacIntyre's answer to the question of flourishing reformulates Aristotle's understanding of the theory of virtue. Drawing on Aristotle's thinking, MacIntyre asserts that virtuous life forms the core of flourishing. To explain flourishing, he introduces the three concepts of (a) practice, (b) narrative unity of human life, and (c) tradition in the teleological structure of virtue (Fives & DiDonato-Barnes, 2013; MacIntyre, 2007). These three elements provide a scheme in which, starting with particular desires of the individual through practice, narrative, and tradition, it becomes possible to search for an answer to the question of what a good and meaningful human life is. MacIntyre believes that "the good life for man is the life spent in seeking for the good life for man" (MacIntyre, 2007, p. 219). In this regard, the end matters as much as the means of achieving that end. Therefore, virtues become the qualities that allow and sustain this quest for the good life of man (Bielskis & Mardosas, 2014). This is the movement toward being "independent practical reasoners" in the theory of practical reasoning. MacIntyre further termed this practical reasoning as *social relations*. He believed that "the networks of giving and receiving" become central in the flourishing community (MacIntyre, 2007, p. 80). Thus, individual flourishing is essentially dependent on other networks within the community from which individuals can receive what they need in order to flourish. Human development is understood, then, as a movement from a condition of intellectual and bodily dependence toward being an "independent practical reasoner." It is the movement from an "initial animal state of having reasons for acting in this way rather than that towards the specifically human state of being able to evaluate those reasons, to revise them or to abandon them and replace them with others" (MacIntyre, 2002, p. 91). Such collective reasoning is what makes the communities of self-scrutiny political: "To reason together about the common good is to reason politically" (MacIntyre, 2002, p. 140). This sets flourishing not just at the individual level but at the organizational level as well. At the organizational level, flourishing requires creating and sustaining social structures and institutions in which the concept of the common good can be meaningfully formulated by members of the organizational community. Such social structures can exist at a level between the family and the state. It is clearly something other than civil society, which is an intermediary between family and the state. Civil society is a place where individuals meet to pursue their private interests. MacIntyre describes the structures where the common good may be articulated, where the questions of the human good, of what makes humans flourish, are asked and answered (Fives & DiDonato-Barnes, 2013).

The second modern approach to flourishing is found in positive psychology (PP). Seligman's work is prominent here. Seligman (2010) contends that the goal of every good life is to flourish; it is actually the goal of any living animal. This thinking also dates back to Aristotle, especially in regard to the belief that eudaimonia is the end goal of human life. However, Seligman's positive psychology moves beyond the good mood approach. Seligman believed, as did Aristotle, that no one would flourish at the expense of personal identity and hedonic well-being. This promotes Aristotle's thinking that "existence is good to the good man, and each man wishes himself what is good, while no one chooses to possess the whole world if he has first to become someone else" (Aristotle, trans. 1984, p. 22). Seligman and his colleagues thus launched a strategy that began with the distinction between pleasant, good, and meaningful lives.

Seligman's (2010) concept of positive psychology aimed at developing interventions that build the enabling conditions of life, not just those that decrease misery. He explained that "positive psychology deals with elements of well-being, which include positive emotion, engagement, relationships, meaning, and accomplishment" (Seligman, 2010, p. 236). Seligman argues that we flourish by living well, and we cannot live well if we lack practical wisdom to engage in virtuous activities. Seligman emphasizes that the goal of positive psychology is simply to help people lead better and good lives. Hence, positive psychology seeks to develop tools to build positive emotions, greater engagement, and an appreciation of meaning in life and its activities (Seligman, 2010). Within the context of living a good life, positive psychology focuses on building resilience, happiness, and optimism in the general population (MacIntyre & Mercer, 2014).

Flourishing has also been a major concern in the field of positive organization behavior (POB). A branch of positive psychology, POB gives prominence to the success and flourishing at the organizational level, with the main objective of understanding what is positive and life-giving in an organization (Baker, 2015; Cameron et al., 2004; Youssef-Morgan & Luthans, 2007). POB studies examine self-efficacy, optimism, hope, resilience, and other personal resources in coping with challenges to organizations (Borji, 2020). In regard to flourishing, POB explores peak performance of an organization by focusing on conditions in which individual employees flourish.

3.2.1 Factors That Influence Flourishing in SENOs

Scholars such as Sepulveda and Salicru (2014) observed that for organizations to flourish, they need to adapt more quickly to all environments and across all functional areas. This is attainable if leaders develop clear and relevant program goals. There is no shortcut approach to flourishing in social enterprises (Salicru, 2014). It takes a deliberate effort by the institution to set up systems and structures that support flourishing in organizations. Sepulveda reported that in early enterprises, commercial activity is primarily undertaken to pursue the social mission of organizations and is embedded within a collective ethos of flourishing. The social economy allows a certain level of distribution of surplus among the direct beneficiaries of organizations, thus adding to fulfillment (flourishing) that employees enjoy.

In addition, Salicru (2014) revealed that not all leaders take advantage of the opportunity presented to them. Few organizations take a deliberate role in the training and development of their workforce. Education, as Aristotle (2000) argued, is necessary in producing happy and productive (flourishing) individuals and society. However, he believed that the ability to recognize opportunities is not equally distributed among people. Opportunities should be anticipated, discovered, and conceptualized in order for them to become operational. According to Aristotle, if one looks for an opportunity without being quite sure what it should be, one should put all one's senses "on watch." The opportunity might come quite unexpectedly, or sometimes under quite strange circumstances. Noteworthy, for Aristotle, is the use of reason as a necessary but not sufficient condition for human flourishing. Living rationally (i.e., consciously) means dealing with the world conceptually. Living consciously implies respect for the facts of reality. This can be attained through proper training, which incites flourishing.

Not only training but interpersonal relationships too are closely linked to flourishing. You cannot talk of one and leave out the other. Epicurus, the fourth-century philosopher, posited that the aim of life is simply to be happy before we dissolve into the atomic universe (before we die). This should bring us to the desire to avoid what is easy to get and the appetite for imminent gratification. The organizations should desist from the desire for artificial stimulation and rather focus on long-term gratification. To Aristotle, flourishing is thus a development implied; flourishing is a process (as previously stated), an activity, a praxis (Hurka, 1999). It combines both subjective and objective goods (De Ruyter, 2007). Organizations mostly overlook the importance of the subjective and objective, the individual experience and collective concerns, and the relational aspects. One can thus not prioritize the individual over the collective. It is startling that modern-day organizational management tends to believe so strongly that the individual is prior to the collective. The point here is that, as an ultra-social species (Fowers, 2015), humans cannot flourish as individuals, only as members of communities. Humans as social beings require community. As Aristotle (trans. 1996) observes in the *Politics*, "Every community is established with a view to some good; for everyone always acts in order to obtain that which they think good" (pp. 1–3). In addition, Aristotle suggested that a community is more than a place where people congregate, exchange goods, and provide common defense. Communities exist, he thought, "for the sake of a good life, and not for the sake of life only" (p. 33). He clarified that "the nature of the polis is to be 0a plurality … a polis is not made up only of so many men, but of different kinds of men; for similar do not constitute a polis" (Aristotle, trans. 1996, pp. 18–25). Individuals thus must look for the common (collective) good in order to achieve the individual good of happiness.

For centuries, leadership has been the center of discussions of the flourishing and effectiveness of any entity. Thus, leadership theories with different philosophical roots have been developed, and other contesting theories continue to emerge at the same time. Leadership theories are most often categorized into four approaches. The trait, behavioral, contingency, and emerging approaches are the four central areas of leadership studies (Glendon & Clarke, 2016; Northouse, 2013; Yukl, 2010). For centuries, we have seen the dominance of competency theories, with practice approaches arising in the past decade.

Poor leadership and management skills are primary factors in failure of enterprises. Therefore, developing leadership is a driving force for enterprise success. One of the central tenets of leadership is the strategic approach. This understanding of the times that organizations are going through calls for a particular leadership style by top managers. This type of leadership will help organizations cope with changes and uncertainty in the general environment. The traditional approach of a leader as a hero or a savior is slowly being replaced with new approaches (Raelin, 2011). Strategic leadership depends to some extent upon how the background and skills of a particular leader fit a firm's unique position. Strategic leadership is essential when we put success of social enterprises into perspective. Two prominent approaches in strategic leadership are transformational and servant leadership.

For strategic leadership, to flourish, social enterprising nonprofit organizations need to have a higher purpose than just making money, a higher purpose which will in turn create a stable cash flow for the organization. Building a strong funding base has been central in creating sustainable and flourishing social enterprises. Although the main focus of any social enterprising organization is human beings, not dollars, the business portion of the organization is really a means to human ends. It is for this reason that social enterprises need both mission and profit-making ventures to sustain their operations. Of course, those two drivers are often in conflict. Mission is the heart of a nonprofit. Unless a nonprofit's social enterprise is truly aligned with its mission, the venture is just another business, albeit one owned and operated by a nonprofit entity (Higgin & Finnie, 2010).

Sepulveda argues that social enterprising nonprofit organizations that strategically position themselves are in a good position to flourish. Strategic positioning of the organization becomes an essential element for flourishing in Sepulveda's understanding of thriving. According to Salicru (2014), organizations that work effectively have a strong overall strategic orientation, alignment, and scope. This is demonstrated through the alignment and integration of the organizational activities with business goals and goals to develop leaders with competencies to grow the business. Flourishing, as noted earlier, is the goal of any nonprofit organization. Still, many organizations languish and die within a short period of operation.

3.3 Challenges in the Operation of SENOs

Many challenges to the African economy hinder flourishing of social enterprising nonprofit organizations (SENOs) in developing countries. These challenges range from the globalization of markets and production to a lack of financial support to poor policies developed by the government to support social entities (Hill, 2009). In addition to these challenges, the information and communication infrastructures in most African countries are weak. Access to these important elements is considered an indispensable condition for widespread socioeconomic development in this age of globalization (Bunzli, 2019).

The market potential for social enterprising in nonprofit organizations in developing countries varies across sectors. Not all sectors are conducive to social enterprises. It should be noted, however, that flourishing, that is, being able to sustain organizational operations in an environment that employees find pleasant and fulfilling, is the ultimate goal of any type of organization, whether it is for-profit or nonprofit. However, not many organizations manage to live in a flourishing state.

There is an active emergent social enterprise scene in developing countries, although few nonprofit organizations identify themselves as SENOs. However, these nonprofit organizations operating social enterprises face several challenges to flourishing in their work. The main ecosystem challenges are uncertainties in the regulatory framework and the lack of adequate financial and nonfinancial support for social enterprising (World Bank, 2017). It is widely believed that the general awareness of the social enterprise concept is low as stated above. There is no clear definition or understanding of the concept, which is perceived as one used primarily by foreign nongovernmental organizations or businesses to attract donor money, not a local concept. Few local nonprofit organizations understand the concept or its benefits, defining themselves as nonprofit or small or medium-size enterprises (Shier et al., 2019; World Bank, 2017).

The budding sector will also accelerate in growth if government creates some form of legal registration for social enterprising or small and medium-size business. The governments in developing countries could incentivize such enterprises with value added tax reductions and other policy benefits, by enhancing access to (grant) financing for social entrepreneurs, and by hosting competitions in specific sectors or on specific development challenges (World Bank, 2017).

Social enterprising nonprofit organizations also face the challenges of unpredictable competitive environments. The unpredictable environment exists in all spheres of economic development. Scholars believe that for the long-term prosperity of businesses, organizations need to have both resilience and sustainability strategies existing symbiotically (Winnard et al., 2017). The resilient conceptual basis is developed from the field of ecology, which looks at the ability of a complex system to return to stability after disruption (Bhamra et al., 2011). Resilience is needed by organizations to cope with turbulent external environments, ranging from smaller agitations to high-impact events (Bhamra et al., 2011; Svensson et al., 2020; Wright et al., 2012). In addition, sustainability is also a system quality. Walker et al. (2002) summarized this as the potential of the SENO to achieve "the continued wellbeing of the economy, society and natural resource base" (Walker et al., 2002, p. 11). Therefore, SENOs should always seek resilient strategies so that they can cope with an unpredictable competitive environment.

Globalization has resulted in markets that were previously historically separate becoming one huge global marketplace. This has presented a new threat to indigenous enterprises in local economies, especially in Africa, in the form of increased competition from foreign entrants. Locally manufactured goods now face intense competition with cheaper quality products from advancing economies like China, India, Brazil, and other countries. The 2009 Business Environment Strengthening Technical Assistance Project report suggested that lack of proper government policies has contributed to SENOs' failure in developing countries. It highlights the fact that low support from the government, high interest rates, cost and custom and excise duty, and unfavorable government policies that give foreign investors an upper hand over indigenous enterprises have all greatly affected the enterprises. Some of the policies in developing countries currently hinder indigenous entrepreneurs from doing well. There is need for governments in developing countries to deliberately develop policies to protect indigenous enterprises.

Clearly, access to finance from financial institutions has been one of the challenges for social enterprises (Shier et al., 2019; Burde et al., 2017; MSME Policy, 2012). It is very hard for many SENOs to access finance from banks and other financial institutions, despite the fact that financial access has been one of the major contributing factors to the flourishing of social entities. The International Finance Corporation (2014) report pointed out that for the 40% of Malawi enterprises that have access to formal financial products, it has proven difficult to meet collateral requirements; high interest rates also discourage borrowing. Research has also shown that high default rates due to political interference have caused several government credit programs to collapse (IFC, 2014).

Furthermore, failure to develop business plans that give an overview of the feasibility of the business has led to challenges for many SENOs. Lack of business education has led many enterprises to operate without a proper business plan (Burde et al., 2017; Moghalu, 2014). This leads to many enterprises' owners spending most of their time handling emergencies because they haven't planned ahead to determine what their responses would be. Laszlo et al. (2012) and Afzal et al. pointed out that enabling individuals to flourish in more than just material or economic terms is becoming a critical challenge for any organization aiming to succeed in complex business environments that increasingly require it to innovate and act in service of its stakeholders. For a business to achieve sustainable flourishing, it will need to catalyze a transformation of its employees and other stakeholders inside and outside the organization to feel, see, be, and act differently. Sustainable flourishing calls for broader perception, a greater sense of connectedness to community and to the rest of the world, and the ability to draw on deeper wisdom, leading to habitual caring for others.

3.4 Chapter Conclusion

Flourishing is the goal of any organization. In Aristotelian philosophy, flourishing is discussed in two dimensions. First, eudemonic well-being is associated with a sense of purpose or meaning in life (Waterman, 1993). It conceptualizes well-being in the cultivation of personal strengths and contribution to the greater good while acting in accordance with inner values in the realization of one's true potential (Aristotle, 2000; Waterman, 1993). Then there is hedonic well-being, which often focuses on the individual degree in the experience of pleasure. It equates well-being with pleasure and happiness (Kahnerman & Tversky, 1999; Ryan & Deci, 2001). Though flourishing is mostly discussed at individual level, there has been recent approach to understand it at organizational level. It is important to investigate comprehensively the state of organizational flourishing through both domains to capture the organizations and employees' strengths and inner values that factor into flourishing, as well as the pleasure and happiness factors that employees of an organization experience.

Chapter 4
A Theory of SENO Flourishing

Over the past years, indigenous nonprofit organizations in Africa have faced challenges in increasing revenue for their work. Consequently, many of them are venturing into social enterprising to increase their income and reduce their dependence on donations. This is connected to the resource dependency school of thought in the operation of social enterprising organizations, which suggests that nonprofit organizations' increased reliance on earned income is associated with cutbacks in philanthropic giving. The decreased government and donor attention to supporting charity organizations is pushing many local nonprofit organizations in Malawi to create new sources of income for their charity work. Essentially, the businesses for nonprofits in Malawi are being created to ensure that such nonprofit organizations are able to raise enough funds for their charity mission and the organization's flourishing.

4.1 Factors Influencing SENOs' Flourishing

The flourishing of social enterprising nonprofit organizations in this study integrates both the classic and modern understanding of flourishing, which I define as the product of the pursuit and engagement of an authentic life that brings inner joy and happiness through meeting goals, being connected with life passion, and relishing accomplishments in the workforce. Understanding flourishing, therefore, demands examining both the individual's experience of pleasure (hedonic well-being) and the contribution to the greater good that comes from living a meaningful and purposeful life (eudaimonic well-being), both of which feed into organizational flourishing. This aligns with Rasmussen's et al. (2011) understanding of flourishing, that happiness is tranquility and enjoyment with commercial society providing the freedom and security that promotes the good life and prevents misery among individuals.

Z. Chijere, *Nonprofit Social Enterprises*, CSR, Sustainability, Ethics & Governance, https://doi.org/10.1007/978-3-031-60234-4_4

Organizational flourishing in both classical and contemporary contexts is community oriented. This study has shown that a social enterprising nonprofit organization is a center of human interrelatedness, and it is this organizational ecosystem that facilitates the flourishing of the organization. Flourishing cannot happen in isolation from the supporting community. To flourish, SENO employees need to be well linked and connected to their hedonic well-being and to their eudaimonic well-being. This creates a community of flourishing. The study reveals the importance of positive interaction within an organization and with forces outside the organization. Most leadership studies have concentrated on organizational interdependency for flourishing (e.g., Allen & Sims, 2018; Brimhall 2019; Graen & Uhl-Bien, 1995; Kram, 1985). Recently, however, some studies have focused on the impact of work relationships in organizational life and an ecosystem of flourishing culture, structure, innovation, and strategies in organizations (Svensson et al., 2020; Trebesch, 2015).

This study focused on identifying factors within the SENO ecosystem that influence their flourishing. These factors, as explained in subsequent chapters, are leadership, organizational culture, human resource management, innovation, market leadership, governance, management, and the way an organization deals with the external environment. I discuss these factors next and develop a model that explains how the factors influence flourishing in these organizations (Table 4.1).

Table 4.1 Flourishing factors

Factor	Description
Leadership	The art of creating vision, stirring innovation, and motivating individuals to achieve intended objectives of the organization by using proactive entrepreneurial behavior that takes advantage of opportunities
Organizational culture	The shared beliefs and values that govern workforce behavior in an organization
Human resource management	The effective recruitment and management of people as an important resource and a center of competitive advantage
Innovation	The creating and/or adopting of new products/services/processes that create efficiency and competitive advantage over other organizations
Market leadership	Being adept at understanding the market and bringing to it the quality of products and services that supersede the standard regulations
Governance	The system of rules, practices, and procedures of conduct that defines the management of an organization
Management	Planning, leading, controlling, organizing, and the day-to-day operations that create an internal organizational environment that helps in goal attainment
The external environment	The ability to understand and build networks with different stakeholders in the external environment of the organization

4.2 The Connection Between Hedonic and Eudaimonic Well-being

A critical analysis of the influence of eight factors in the operations of SENOs shows that flourishing springs from these factors feeding into both hedonic well-being and eudaimonic well-being. Hedonic well-being often focuses on the experience of pleasure, hence equating well-being with pleasure, happiness, and fulfillment (Shier et al., 2019; Borji, 2020; Kahnerman & Tversky, 1999; Ryan & Deci, 2001). On the other hand, eudaimonic well-being focuses on the experience of purpose and meaning. It conceptualizes well-being in the cultivation of personal strengths and contribution to the greater good while acting in accordance with inner values in the realization of one's true potential (Aristotle, trans. 2000; Waterman, 1993). When individuals experience both hedonic and eudaimonic well-being within their work environment, they give their best in serving in an organization. Individuals' positive experience translates into organizational flourishing. My interviews with SENOs' founders, directors, and managers revealed that these SENO leaders look for both experience of the good life (hedonic well-being) and the achievement of purpose and meaning (eudaimonic well-being). To understand how and why organizations flourish, there is a need to understand the workforce experience of pleasure and fulfillment (hedonic well-being) and the contribution to the greater good in living a meaningful and purposeful life (eudaimonic well-being). I contend that the hedonic well-being of the individuals creates the hedonic well-being for an organization. Happy workforces craft happy organizations. This, in turn, helps the organizations to function well. Similarly, the well-functioning organization creates a feeling good within the social enterprising nonprofit organization.

4.2.1 *The Flourishing Ecosystem*

SENO flourishing resides in an ecosystem which comprises both hedonic and eudaimonic well-beings. As Stam and Spigel (2016), cited in Tuber (2019), argue, the success and productivity of social entrepreneurship (social enterprising is what social entrepreneurs do) in a certain territory hinge on a set of factors as well as interdependent actors that operate within what is called the entrepreneurship ecosystem. Tuber (2019) further posited that this ecosystem in turn is influenced by government policies, private and public sector support, access to human capital, access to financial capital, the market, and the culture that influences an enterprise's function and success. That is why Cooper (2015) called for organizations to be creating strategies linked to the bottom line. In such situations, organizations should look for and draw on both intangible and tangible factors such as culture and leadership. These feed into organizational flourishing, the level that influences the ability of an organization to carry out its mission. Organizational flourishing thus is about increasing an organization's workforce's ability to experience pleasure and sustain

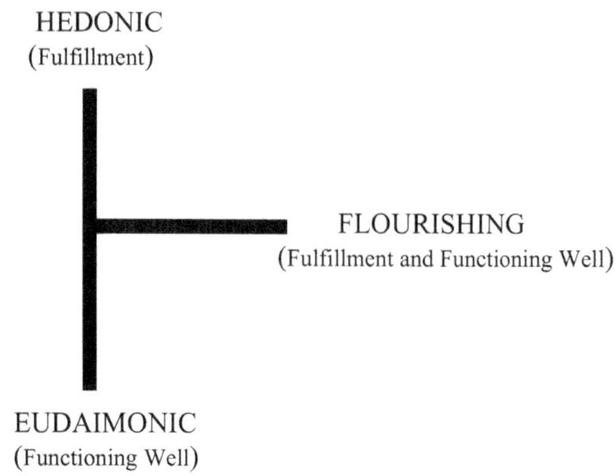

Fig. 4.1 Symbiotic relationship between hedonic and eudaimonic well-beings

long-term goals. Flourishing happens in an organization when the organization is able to create a fulfilling working environment that supports the functioning well of the organization and vice versa.

Figure 4.1 illustrates this symbiotic relationship of hedonic and eudaimonic well-beings with respect to the flourishing of an organization.

Flourishing organizations have high levels of both eudaimonic well-being and hedonic well-being. Eudaimonic well-being is associated with a sense of purpose or meaning in life (Waterman, 1993). It conceptualizes well-being in the cultivation of personal strengths and contribution to the greater good while acting in accordance with inner values in the realization of one's true potential (Aristotle, 2000; Waterman, 1993). Hedonic well-being, on the other hand, often focuses on the individual's experience of pleasure, equating well-being with pleasure and happiness (Kahnerman & Tversky, 1999; Ryan & Deci, 2001). An individual experiencing hedonic well-being and enjoying eudaimonic well-being would be fulfilled and have a clear sense of purpose or meaning in life. An individual's flourishing occurs when there is a good connection between the hedonic and the eudaimonic well-being. Such an individual (a fulfilled and purpose-driven one) is a prime asset to an organization, contributing to flourishing of an organization. SENOs that pursue both hedonic well-being and eudaimonic well-being of employees would thus experience a higher level of flourishing.

4.2.2 The SENO Flourishing Model

Following is a brief discussion of how each of these factors contributes either to the feeling good (hedonic well-being) or the functioning well (eudaimonic well-being) of the organization. The first issue is how these factors contribute to both the hedonic and eudaimonic well-being of an organization's workforce (which contribute to organizational flourishing) and how the hedonic-eudaimonic well-being combo advances SENO flourishing. Figure 4.2 illustrates the flourishing model for social

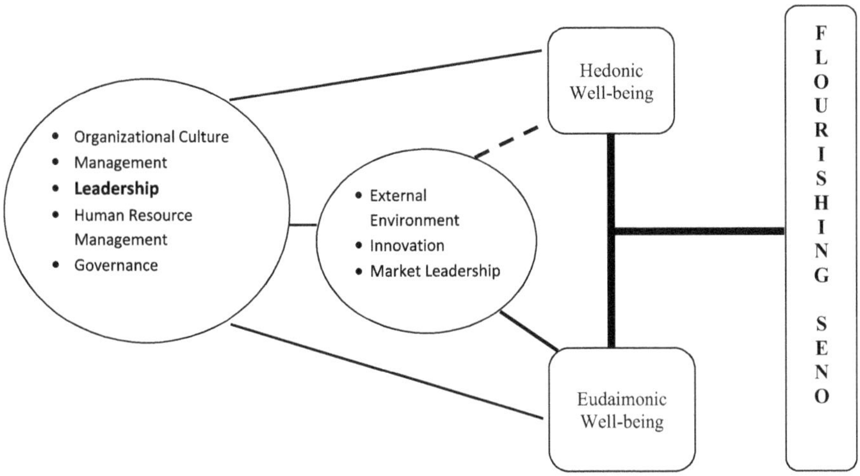

Fig. 4.2 The SENO flourishing modelNote:The bold line represents strong influencerThe dotted lines represent weak influencerThe bold letters represent the most dominant factors

enterprising nonprofit organizations. It depicts the factors that influence hedonic and eudaimonic well-being and how a combination of these well-beings leads to flourishing in a SENO. Hedonic well-being is concerned with the internal health of the organization and ensuring that the workforce is motivated, valued, inspired, and engaged in creating a workforce community of fulfilled employees. Of noteworthiness here, for SENOs, flourishing is not only seen in growing the charity work and recording profits in the social enterprise but also in the quality of the organization's internal life and climate. The key issue in regard to hedonic well-being is for SENOs to create an internal organizational system that is healthy and functioning in the process of achieving the organization's objectives. Eudaimonic well-being, on the other hand, focuses on the functioning well of the organization, the optimal performance of the organization. This is linked to a workforce enjoying hedonic well-being. Understandably, both hedonic and eudaimonic well-being factors feed into SENO flourishing.

This section first explains how each of the eight factors create a feeling good and/or functioning well experience and then explains how workforce well-being feeds into SENO flourishing.

Organizational rules, practices, and procedures of conduct are critical for both hedonic and eudaimonic well-being. Governance is thus important here; it has strong influence represented by the thick continuous lines to both hedonic and eudaimonic well-being. Governance is concerned with the whole structure of the organization. This ranges from visioning to the design of the organization. A clear governance system helps the SENO have clear guidelines, which guide the organization's operations. Furthermore, the governance structure guides the organization in aligning the vision with the internal organizational environment. In addition, proper governance systems for SENOs facilitate the authentic engagement of individuals in the organization, which is vital in creating a good organizational climate. The flourishing organization has clear operational procedures that have been key to the creation of trust within the organization and with the outside stakeholders.

Effective governance allows for efficient day-to-day management, therefore also strongly influencing both hedonic and eudaimonic well-being. The day-to-day operations are critical for creating a positive organizational climate for hedonic well-being, which leads to effective functioning of organizations. The day-to-day running of an organization engages in transforming long-term goals into concrete plans of action for the workforce to implement. Further, this day-to-day management of the organization helps to align the goals to the overall strategy of the organization, which is essential in the functioning well of the organization. For the SENO, this gives proper direction on the day-to-day behavior of the organization. The flourishing organization emphasizes clear action, which originates from the core vision of the organization. Therefore, management of flourishing SENOs focuses on positive engagement of the workforce which in turn promotes organizational citizenship behavior, the kind of behavior in which the employees identify the organization as theirs. This positively influences the commitment of the workforce to the organization. Just as suggested by POB, SENOs explore peak performance of an organization by focusing on conditions in which individual employees flourish through the creation of clear conditions of operation. A well-crafted organization's day-to-day management system guides the organization's workforce into feeling good, which increases their commitment to the organization, thus enabling it to function well.

Just as in governance and management, leadership has a strong link to both hedonic well-being and eudaimonic well-being. Leadership that adds value is central to SENO flourishing. Leadership is a dominant factor. In the analysis of the data, leadership was found to be a prerequisite to all other factors. Leadership has the role of creating an organization's vision, developing strategies and goals, and then transforming these into action plans. As earlier discussed, strategic leadership is the potential of leaders to express a strategic vision to motivate and persuade followers. This involves a deeper level of analytical thinking in leading dual-mission organizations. The flourishing SENO knows that leadership is a crucial factor in creating an environment where the workforce is able to think of creative approaches that will promote success. Strategic leadership and thinking help the organization to focus on the environmental variables that lead the organization to create a conducive work environment and at the same time live the optimal purpose of the organization.

Vision cannot be achieved unless there is the right type of human capital in an organization. Recruiting the right people for the right positions, which, for some of the SENOs studied, involved supporting the education of people who would later join the organization, is undertaken by the human resource departments. This human resource management strongly influences both the hedonic and eudaimonic well-being of SENOs. Human resource management focuses on the physical, mental, and social health of the employees. The goal here is to get the right people into the right positions and ensure that they are trained and challenged. Flourishing SENOs focus on developing the workforce through training. As highlighted in Aristotle's notion of well-being, we become better through practice and become more virtuous through education and habit. The pursuit of knowledge is central for organization flourishing. The SENOs studied initiated several HRM development approaches within their systems to help in the gaining of knowledge, skills, and abilities so the organizations can achieve their goals. The flourishing SENOs focus on fostering creativity in the organization by first recognizing and then acknowledging, supporting, and rewarding employees' accomplishments.

The management of human resources influences an organization's culture, the organization's values, beliefs, and ethics that define the type of relationships (good or bad) in the organization. An organization's culture has a strong link with both hedonic and eudaimonic well-being. Flourishing is achieved through relationships in the workplace. Leaders focus on creating an organizational culture based on the virtues and values that enhance relationships within the organization. Ethical conduct has been a central concept in creating a culture that propels the organization to success because it creates trust in the work environment. Values and organizational justice promote the virtues of courage, innovation, hard work, and engagement, which are essential in the performance of the organization. Aristotle indicates that man is a rational creature who lives in society, which calls for relational environment. Organizational culture is central to a well-lived life because it enables a good working environment in which employees can be innovative and motivated to do the work.

A positive work environment stirs innovation, which has a strong link with eudaimonic well-being because it is critical to new ideas being introduced in the functioning of an organization. Innovation on the other hand has only weak influence on hedonic well-being because it may not always lead to being fulfilled; sometimes it can be a source of anxiety. Organizational innovation and creativity are enacted in a SENO with the aim of creating social and economic value in the products/services. Managers invest in the organization's creativity in order to transform ideas into products or services that meet the required standards of both their charity work and their social enterprising. The ability to innovate and initiate a culture of continuous innovation has been at the center of making SENOs relevant in their charity and social enterprising work. The attitude toward an experimenting orientation (trying new ideas) is high in the flourishing SENO that allows individuals to experiment with certain ideas in their work. Interviews with several organizations showed a balance in culture and commitment toward giving room to employees with experimental ideas, which helps in creating a sustainable and differentiated market position. The flourishing SENOs hire creative staff and invest in their training. Further, SENOs that are flourishing see the values of research and development in getting market information, which positively influences their innovative behaviors. Several flourishing SENOs in this study invest in doing research in order to be unique in their products or services. They do not just venture into the environment without proper knowledge of what works and what does not work.

Innovative SENOs also tend to be market leaders in their area of service, whether charity or social enterprising. Because of reasons similar to those discussed under innovation, market leadership has a strong link with eudaimonic well-being but a weak link with the hedonic well-being since market leadership occurs basically in response to the external environment. SENOs focus on market leadership through quality products and/or services. The flourishing SENO focuses on creating an image that helps them to win customers' loyalty while maintaining good functioning in their dual missions. In this, they focus on the service/product development processes that have strong connections with the mission and their customers. The core mission of the SENO becomes the driving force in creating an image that will give them a good market share of their products and services. The ability to create quality and maintain the customer base on top of selecting a unique industry creates the acceptability of their products/services, driving the SENO toward flourishing. Porter's (1985) competitive advantage model is central to the market leadership orientation of SENOs. The flourishing SENO has a clear focus on its business approach. On top of that, market leadership demands that SENOs focus on differentiation both in the quality of their products and in their business niche. This helps the organization gain a market position that gives them a strategic advantage over their competitors. This ability to control the behavior of the market has been essential in the flourishing of SENOs.

Market leadership is basically external-oriented. Managing the external environment is a critical factor in leadership. This factor strongly influences eudaimonic well-being but has only a weak influence over hedonic well-being since the organization focuses mainly on how to deal with external forces. The organizations in this study understand that to function well they need to have a strong network with government agencies and other critical organizations in fulfilling their goals. The SENO that is able to make good relationships and networks with political powers will get government support for their work, a vital element in achieving optimum performance. As Aristotle argues, humans cannot flourish as individuals, only as members of a community. The flourishing SENOs strategically include the government in their plans of work. Government (as well as other organizations they may choose to partner with) is part of the organizations' community. Such partnerships and consultations provide social networks, which are important enabling forces for SENOs to achieve their dual-mission (charity and social enterprising) goals. In working alongside other partners, flourishing SENOs create consortiums within their industry that support the work of the organization. High levels of dependability make an organization more likely to flourish (Schotanus-Dijkstra, 2016).

Flourishing is not just achieving the goals of the organization but also members living well as their organization strives to achieve its goals. Just as in positive psychology, SENOs that are flourishing focus on pleasant, good, and meaningful life by creating an environment for the workforce to identify with and have a sense of belonging to the organization. As highlighted in the previous section, they focus on creating enabling conditions of life that decrease misery while increasing greater engagement of employees as they meet the goals of their organization. Therefore, for SENOs, flourishing combines the organization both functioning well and living well, as highlighted at the beginning of the chapter. In this regard, both living well and functioning well depend on the networks of giving and receiving which create a strong social relationship both within and outside of the organization that facilitates good life for the hybrid (charity and business) organization. This good life, just as in POB, is positive and life giving to the organization (Baker, 2015). This means that leaders in flourishing SENOs create a reflective organization that is able to assess itself while they focus on achieving the full potential of the organization by creating conducive organizational climate. Good performance of the organization, therefore, is seen by creating conditions in which the individual is able to flourish. The leaders thus strive to create sustainable social structures and institutions which are essential in creating such hedonic environment. In turn, the hedonic environment improves workforce identity and belonging to the organization and facilitates greater engagement among the employees, and this feeds into eudaimonic well-being.

Organizations are living organisms created and developed by individuals who continually strive for peak performance of their organization. Peak organizational performance has been the central concept in positive organizational behavior (POB) (Baker, 2015; Parker, 2019). Peak organizational performance calls for positive engagement of employees in order to advance flourishing. To achieve this, employees' contribution in the organizations is critical to the output of the organization. This means that positive engagement, both physical and emotional, is very important in the flourishing of a hybrid organization. The ability to learn, develop, align, execute, and renew faster than competitors has been a goal for many flourishing SENOs. This is possible in the organizational climate that promotes positive citizenship behavior of the employees. The SENO's internal organizational climate becomes so essential in the operation of the hybrid organization because it is this climate that sustains the performance of the organization. Therefore, the hedonic well-being and eudaimonic well-being create an entrepreneurial ecosystem that promotes the interdependency of the charity and business ventures that is essential in the flourishing of the hybrid organizations.

Figure 4.3 indicates the theoretical diagram on how the hedonic well-being combines with the eudemonic well-being in the flourishing of social enterprising nonprofit organizations. The organization needs to experience a good health in three major elements identified in Fig. 4.3. It is the combination of these hedonic and eudemonic well-being that drives the organizations into flourishing. Flourishing doesn't just happen for the social enterprising nonprofit organizations; it is a process that requires deliberate action to be attained.

4.2.3 Connecting the Flourishing Factors

The SENO flourishing process was modeled in Fig. 4.2. This model represents how the eight factors identified in this research influence both hedonic and eudaimonic well-being. These eight factors complement each other, and the good health of each determines the health of others in advancing flourishing in a SENO. They are the building blocks of SENO flourishing. All these factors/building blocks, both hedonic and eudaimonic well-being, need to be present in good health for the organization

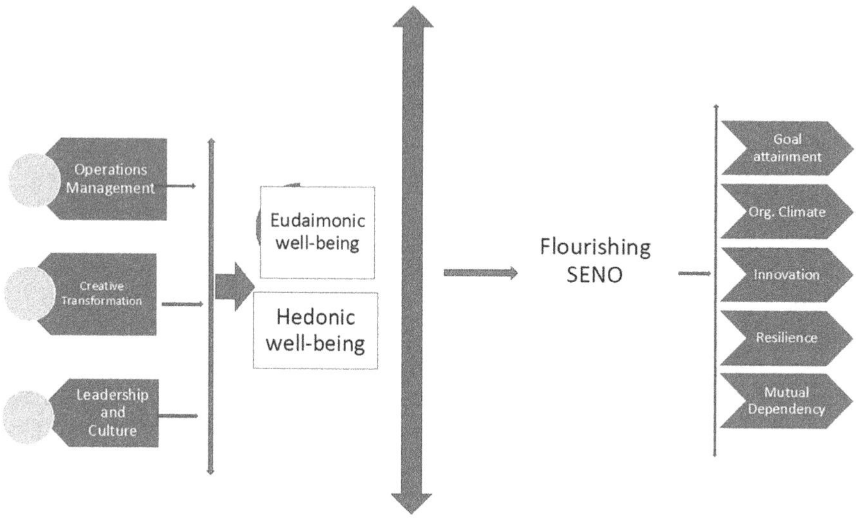

Fig. 4.3 The SENO flourishing theoretical diagram

to flourish. The hedonic well-being factors create a feel-good organizational climate, thus influencing the work behavior of the individuals in the organization. The organizational climate that relieves distress and promotes happiness in the workforce is essential in the flourishing of the organization. The hedonic factors promote workforce self-efficacy, innovative behavior, and the organizational citizenship behaviors which are important in the achievement of organizational goals. The enjoyment felt by the individuals in the organization promotes their work achievement.

The eudaimonic well-being factors, on the other hand, focus on the meaning and purpose of the organization, that is, why the organization exists. They facilitate the fulfillment of the organization's existence. Eudaimonic factors, therefore, help the organization achieve its purpose. Some of the building blocks can have a strong link to either of the two well-beings, while others are strongly linked with both of the well-beings. In addition, the other building blocks have a weak link to either hedonic or eudaimonic well-being. This indicates that SENO flourishing is a multidimensional construct that encompasses a variety of hedonic and eudaimonic well-being factors that need to be in good health for the flourishing of the organization. SENOs reach their peak by creating a eudaimonic environment while focusing on the conditions in which the individuals flourish, the hedonic well-being.

There is a cross-sectional association between living a good life and functioning well in the flourishing SENO. Hedonism and eudaimonia are two distinct but related philosophies. Thus, instead of focusing on one well-being as more important than the other, SENO flourishing depends on both of these well-beings. Both the experience of pleasure and the experience of meaning are what leads to SENO flourishing. That suggests that there would be little flourishing when one dimension of well-being is overlooked. The hedonic factors such as governance, leadership, culture, human resource, and management are essential in creating an internal system that promotes workforce identity with the organization, joy, and engagement. The individual well-being increases the workforce contribution in the performance of the organization. Flourishing SENOs hence tend to focus on creating a motivated workforce and a good organizational climate that will promote positive engagement of the workforce. The hedonic dimension leads the individuals to the positive psychological functioning in which they become more committed, engaged, and innovative in their work. In addition, hedonic well-being provides an internal organizational climate that creates a satisfying environment for the workforce. The organizational internal climate plays a vital role in creating a happy working environment which stirs the workforce into creativity, innovation, and positive organizational citizenship behavior that becomes essential in achieving full potential. This is the eudaimonia of the organization in which service is honorable.

The eudaimonic well-being factors such as external environment, market leadership, innovation, and management create a learning organization in pursuit of excellence when competing with other organizations. Eudaimonia enables organizations to achieve the purpose of their existence. These eudaimonic building blocks/factors help the organization focus on achieving its goals for existence. In other words, the functioning well of a SENO is facilitated by those factors that enable the organization to achieve its mission. Eudaimonia also helps in mitigating the tensions of hybridity by clearly stating how the charity and business venture can mutually support each other. In functioning well, the organization reaches optimum performance both in the charity and the for-profit side of the organization.

There is the unbreakable connection between hedonic and eudaimonic well-being that leads to a flourishing organization. Functioning well feeds into feeling good and vice versa. Anything less is associated with a greater burden in balancing the structural and mission differences of the charity and business venture. Feeling good and the functioning well consistently overlap in the operation of the hybrid organization that is flourishing. Such flourishing can only happen when an organization experiences a good level of health for each dimension; these factors are interconnected and interrelated and influence each other. It is this interconnectedness that creates pleasure and wholesomeness in the life of an organization's workforce and in achieving its intended goals.

Flourishing SENOs create a happier living and a well-functioning hybrid organization. There is a reciprocal and associational relationship between the flourishing of the organization and the factors that bring that flourishing. This means that there is a backward influence in the SENO flourishing model. The flourishing organization facilitates an organization with more living good and more functioning well. Flourishing is linked with creating organizational resilience, improved happiness, creativity, and organizational citizenship behavior. Beyond this, flourishing creates a more conducive environment for the belonging, engagement, relationships, meaning, and accomplishment so essential to the organizational workforce's experiencing of meaning and pleasure. Therefore, hedonic well-being factors in a SENO are robustly associated with the eudaimonic well-being factors.

Understandably, there is tension between the charity and business sides of SENOs, and flourishing SENOs have to deal with this tension between charity and business goals.

4.3 Dealing with Charity-Business Tension

The dual goals of SENOs, charity and business, characterize these organizations as hybrids and set particular challenges in their operation. At the same time, SENOs need to manage multiple stakeholders' demands of these two almost competing sides. The flourishing SENOs hence have to balance the tensions that arise. Balancing the charity and business sides is one of the greatest challenges that can compromise flourishing in hybrid organizations. Competing goals pose a management and governance challenge to these SENOs. Figure 4.4 illustrates the hybridity and the tension this hybridity brings forth.

As SENOs seek to achieve both their charity and business (social enterprising) goals, they engage in a blended approach in their management and leadership. Leaders try to ensure that the nonprofit and business sides depend on each other and that the charity and business sides exist for each other. This demands proper procedures to be set in place so that the profits are effectively generated and are properly invested into the social mission or charity.

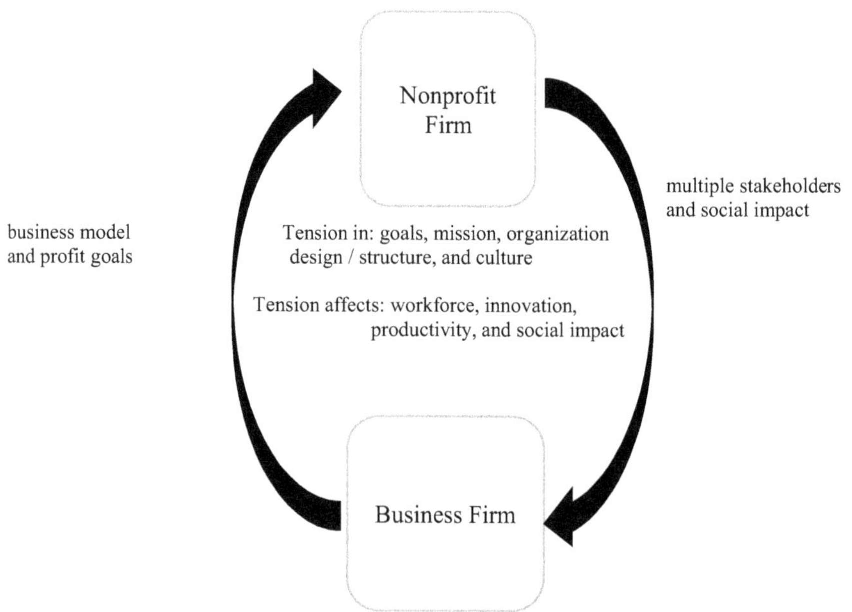

Fig. 4.4 Balancing hybridity tension in SENOs

There are trade-offs in avoiding the social mission drift where the social mission is overlooked. There have been situations where the SENOs reported that they were at risk of diverging from the charity toward the business mission, times when the business venture outgrew the social mission entity. The probability of mission drift is very high in a SENO, especially when there are no deliberate blended governance and management approaches. Hybridity can compromise flourishing; this seems to be common when only one side of the hybrid organization is doing very well. A tight connection between the two is essential in reducing the tension that comes with the hybridity of the organization. This demands that leaders be passionate about linking the charity and business missions of SENOs.

Other organizations overcome the tension by sectionalization. This is when both the charity and the business ventures take their own identities in their operations. This is done by creating two organizations that are mutually dependent on each other but have separate operation systems. The study uncovered that this helps in reducing the conflict in values, mission, goals, and management of the business and charity ventures. In this situation, there isn't direct overplay of activities in the ventures. Each venture makes its own decisions regarding day-to-day operations without consulting the other. This option helps the charity and the business ventures to operate as they ought to. In their existence, they complement each other in the overall strategy, but this requires leadership committed to ensuring success of both the charity and business sides.

4.3.1 *The Flourishing Unbreakable Relationship*

There exist significant interactions between factors, what I consider the building blocks, of flourishing of a SENO. The internal factors, those influencing what is happening in the organization (leadership, management, human resource management, governance, and the organizational culture), feed into each other but also influence the externally focused factors (market leadership, innovation, and external environment). Analysis suggests that these factors influence hedonic well-being and eudaimonic well-being strongly but differently. The internal factors influence what happens in the organization; they have strong influence over both hedonic well-being and eudaimonic well-being. On the other hand, externally focused factors have a strong influence over eudaimonic well-being but a weak influence over hedonic well-being. Contextually, it seems that flourishing in SENOs is not organic; it does not just emerge. It is a well-crafted and intentional approach that combines good health in all the identified flourishing factors. Beyond that, flourishing includes healthy coexistence of the nonprofit and business sides.

Flourishing for a dual-mission organization moves beyond happiness, combining several positive psychology constructs that create a more holistic perspective of what it means to live happily and to achieve organizational goals. The context of flourishing of each SENO rests on how it approaches its hedonic and eudaimonic well-being domains. The ability for peak functioning is necessitated by feeling good (hedonic well-being) within the organization achieved through an organizational climate that is positive for the workforce to live a fulfilling life. When fulfilled, the workforce becomes very productive.

When defining flourishing, both well-beings need to be taken into account. To flourish, the SENO needs good health both in the workforce experience of the good life (hedonic well-being) and in the workforce commitment to achieve the organization's purpose and meaning (eudaimonic well-being). Instead of focusing on one over the other, flourishing for the SENO necessitates drawing on both sides of well-being. It is essential for SENOs to understand that both domains of well-being are essential. Flourishing for dual-mission nonprofit organizations demands that organizations focus on experience of pleasure of the workforce (hedonic well-being) and contribution to the greater good in living a meaningful and purposeful life (eudaimonic well-being). This is done through promoting the internal health of the organization that enables the workforce to be committed. Feeling good and functioning well must both be attained for an organization to flourish. When one is emphasized over the other, the well-being of the organization could be hindered.

Context-wise, SENO flourishing is not an activity nor a trait or fixed event. It is a curated culture that yields sound internal organization linking the internal and external factors so as to spur efficient operations and goal attainment. Thus, the goal for any dual-mission organization is to achieve optimum organizational functioning and maximal performance both for its charity and its social enterprising ventures. The flourishing SENO thus seeks to maintain an internal system that creates a good organizational climate facilitating success and positive interaction with the external environment.

Just as in positive psychology, the flourishing SENO aims at developing interventions that build enabling conditions of life for individuals working in an organization—not just interventions that decrease misery for the workforce but ones that help the employees to be happy as they do their work. Participants in this study emphasized deliberate effort in creating a reward system that benefits even the bottom-level employees. Beyond the reward system, the SENOs also focused on employees' independence and interdependence in doing their work. They realized that creativity is only promoted when the workforce is allowed to experiment with their ideas while also interacting with one another.

As Aristotle observed, people feel happy if they experience life's purpose, challenges, and growth together; this has been a focus for flourishing in the SENOs studied. They prioritized human relations and a life governed by reason and excellence of character—a life of rational activity done in accordance with virtue. Scholars such as Annas (2011), Borji (2020), argue that flourishing goes beyond the things we own; it is a matter of how well we live our lives. Living our lives well is developing our capabilities to achieve worthwhile goals.

Chapter 5
Operations Management

Operations management is the business practice that is concerned with translating, as efficiently as possible, raw material and labor into an end product or service to maximize the success of an organization. Operations management of the social enterprising nonprofit organizations (SENOs) has been one of the crucial issues in flourishing. Operations management was regarded by the research participants in this study as the element that helps build the capabilities of the organizations to achieve their visions and missions.

Management is concerned with planning, leading, organizing, and controlling the resources and activities of an organization in order to convert the raw materials and labor into products and/or services that satisfy the stakeholders' needs. The findings suggest that good management is one of the central tenets in the operation and subsequent success and flourishing of a SENO. Because of the dual bottom-line nature of SENOs, balancing the competing goals in the way they are managed is critical. The SENOs are consistently called upon to balance the business goals and the charity goals.

5.1 Balancing Two Competing Organizational Goals

The study's findings revealed that management of hybrid organizations poses a unique challenge to most leaders and managers. The SENOs are regarded as hybrid organizations because they mix elements, value systems, and goals of both private sector and the charity sector. A particular challenge for SENOs is that they are hybrid in nature: they must both fulfill their social mission and make a profit. SENO management must thus manage both the profit and nonprofit activities in a dual bottom-line organization. This calls for prudent management of the tension that exists between the for-profit and the nonprofit propositions within the governance

Z. Chijere, *Nonprofit Social Enterprises*, CSR, Sustainability, Ethics & Governance, https://doi.org/10.1007/978-3-031-60234-4_5

natures of the two. Ménard (2004) described SENOs as institutional "weirdos" because of the tension brought by their dual goal nature.

The hybridity of pursuing social mission goals while at the same time generating resources to be used in pursuit of the social mission can bring conflicts within the organization. The founders interviewed shared that these conflicts range from resource allocation to management style of the entity. That is why the interviewees suggested that the management systems in SENO must integrate the dual goals if they are to be successful. The study uncovered the fact that the SENO that deliberately focuses on setting up systems that will facilitate the smooth operation of both the charity and for-profit ventures is more successful in its operations. Interviews and observations revealed that successful SENOs create boundaries between resource creation and mission-driven goals in order to reduce this tension. The boundary helps the entities to know clearly what is expected from the enterprise and from the charity. To this end, the managers understand that they cannot use only a single management approach in managing the organizations.

5.1.1 Dealing with Enterprise Profits or Loss

Some managers explained that, as they pursue social and financial returns simultaneously, they set different management systems. Mike, the Executive Director of CAISD, shared that "The way we manage the nonprofit is different from the way we manage the enterprise because the goals are different. We need to make money in the enterprise, so we design the enterprise in the way that we are able to bring money." This means that setting up different management systems has helped the organizations to understand clearly how they would increase profit margins while pursuing social goals. The SENOs strive to separate the management system of the nonprofit from that of the for-profit entity in their operational strategy. Commenting on this, Phillip, a manager of Media, Networking, and Communication at CYON, indicated that since the for-profit and the nonprofit entities seek different goals, it becomes essential to clearly set up different management systems that will guide the management of the SENO.

Some organizations in this study have one management system for both the business and the charity venture. Others in the management of such SENOs agree that this hinders the growth of both the charity and the enterprise, especially if one person is making the decisions. In addition, the two entities require different skills, abilities, and knowledge bases in their management. This is in agreement with the literature on successful management of dual bottom-line organizations. Lee et al. raised the same issues, pointing out that conflict may arise from the pursuit of dual and competing missions if the managers fail to differentiate the operations of the two, since they draw values, norms, and practices from antithetical institutionalized forms of organization, thus creating dual goal tension.

Most founders in this study constantly highlighted their ability to balance the distribution of resources between the nonprofit and the for-profit ventures in managing dual bottom-line organizations. It was observed that successful SENOs have a well-balanced approach to allocating resources for both the for-profit and the nonprofit. One founder shared that some years ago, they faced big survival challenges due to the poor allocation of resources between the charity and the enterprise. The leadership was investing a lot of money in the enterprise and forgetting the charity work; they had well-qualified personnel in the enterprise while overlooking the charity work. This indicates the peril that dual-mission organizations face in failing to allocate resources appropriately. In this founder's case, this led the enterprise to outgrow the charity work. However, when the enterprise began to decline, it affected the operations of the charity as well. A good balance in growing the business while at the same time using the profits wisely for the charity work has helped many social enterprising organizations to grow. Luke, CDECO Executive Director, further remarked:

> There is a need to have a very good understanding of the different principles that guide the operation of these two entities, and also the understanding of where these two entities merge, because in its essence these two are meant to be a support to each other. We work on balancing the two because our core mandate is the charity work; the companies came in because we wanted to raise money to finance our charity work. We don't want to forget our charity work and only concentrate on the companies.

In addition, it was observed that many leaders strive to create procedures and management policies that help proper distribution of scarce resources within the SENO. Proper resource distribution is one measure that has helped many SENOs to control the mission drift from social mission to entirely business. For instance, one participant indicated that there was a time when their social enterprise grew bigger than the nonprofit activities because more resources and effort were directed to the business rather than the nonprofit. That raised the question of "why do we exist," seeing that the charity work was almost nonessential. Therefore, proper resource distribution for social and financial goals is an increasingly important element in helping the SENO grow and flourish. One such element is that many SENOs have a clear definition of how much of their profit is put into charity work and how much is reinvested into the company. Mike shared that they make sure that 60% of their profits are put into charity work. This helps the SENO to fulfill their mission of generating money through business ventures to support the charity work.

Most founders also raised the role of abilities, skills, and knowledge in managing dual-mission organizations. The findings show that these elements have been a central factor in the SENOs that are surviving. It was discovered that the capability of leadership to successfully operate two entities with different aims has the potential to help the success of the organization. Peter of Care Malawi shared that SENOs need to run the enterprise as a business and the nonprofit as a charity, thus calling for individuals who are conversant with the two. The findings reveal that when managers without knowledge and skills in running a business choose to lead a SENO, it becomes a disaster. The research participants constantly shared that individuals can't run a SENO with only a charitable mind. Luke, a founder of CDECO, remarked that they had made the mistake of taking all the charity leaders when the enterprise was starting and making them managers in the SENO. He explained:

> We had people with no idea on the business principles running the enterprise. We went bankrupt, both the enterprise and the charity. We almost closed the organizations; we were losing it. Then we thought of changing the business approach. We employed individuals with a good track record in business and those who were trained to manage profit-making companies. We managed to save the company and nonprofit. So, I would say, "Let individuals with business knowledge run the enterprise."

This resonates with several scholars, such as Yasanthi, Haeffele and Storr (2019), and Suykens et al. (2021), who contend that, in blended value creation, success depends on effective management of dual objectives. This is in line with this study's findings that show that the coexistence of equally significant social and financial objectives should be clearly understood by the manager of any dual-mission organization. Adding to this, scholars like Grossi et al. (2017) call for incorporation of structural elements from two types of organizations that are essentially antithetical. Flourishing organizations vary in their management styles, since they know that for-profit and nonprofit ventures will require different skills and capabilities in order to be successful. Leaders must be entrepreneurial.

5.2 Developing an Entrepreneurial Mindset for Leaders

Leaders and managers need to develop an entrepreneurial mindset as an essential element in "happy living" for their organization. The *Financial Times* (2019) referred to the entrepreneurial mindset as a specific state of mind that orients human conduct toward entrepreneurial activities and outcomes. This is the ability to see an opportunity in the community and make best use of that opportunity. It involves creativity to overcome challenges in the operation of the organization. This study's findings suggest that the management of SENOs calls for creativity and innovation at the center of any entrepreneurial organization. Most founders suggested that this requires the SENO leaders to adopt an entrepreneurial mindset in their thinking and vision implementation. The business entrepreneurial approaches and outcomes by the management team are essential in the success of the SENO, since they help in maximizing profits and increase revenue for the charity, which is the basic purpose of running a social enterprise.

Two categories of mindsets are essential in entrepreneurial ventures that are observed in successful SENOs. These are termed by Mathisen (2013) as the elaborating mindset and the implementing mindset. The elaborating mindset is the prerequisite to starting a for-profit venture, and the implementing mindset is the thinking process required to identify and set out strategies to achieve the objectives of the venture. Elaborative mindset in this study is the ability to be open to new information and becoming attentive in creating new ideas. The ability to gain both the elaborating and implementing mindsets has been the distinguishing mark of flourishing organizations. The ability to start and implement activities is a central aspect of entrepreneurial organizations. The interviewees believed that having these two kinds of mindset is essential to running successful entrepreneurial organizations. An entrepreneurial mentality is developed through several approaches. This study has identified that training of the management team to be entrepreneurial in both nonprofit and for-profit ventures is a critical factor in the flourishing of SENOs. For instance, Henry of MSAHI explained that formal and informal training of the staff running the organization is essential in helping the staff to develop the tactical mindset to be innovative in their approaches. The SENO's goals go beyond social impact; it has to make profits that will help the operations of the charity work. Henry further believed that this cannot be possible without having a trained workforce with a mindset that is able to be thoughtful and creative. On the importance of training the workforce to gain entrepreneurial thinking, Linda of Hope Inc. remarked, "Trainings change how the officers approach work. Now we are making high standard products and at the same time, we do focus on the profitability of the company. This has also helped us to meet the targets in production." Additionally, the founder of CSE explained:

> Training even for the leaders is important for them to think as businesspeople. It is easy to motivate the staff if you know and believe what you are doing. I see that many nonprofit organizations start social enterprises without any basic understanding of what it means to run a business.

Strong knowledge of the entrepreneurial processes is clearly an essential element in the management of successful SENOs, since leaders are challenged to be more creative and innovative in their operations. SENOs that fail to manage such processes do not survive in their industry because they waste resources and incur losses, which in the end affects both the charity and the business objectives. Therefore, managing the entrepreneurial processes of innovation and creativity well is a skill that SENO leaders need to acquire if they want to be successful. Titus of Tonga Foundation observed:

> I head the running of the business as well as the running of the foundation. But most of the times I am in the foundation side because we have got managers who are running the lodge. I realized that I need people who know how to run businesses to take control of the business side. I have been in the nonprofit world the whole of my career; I needed some people who would help me to think like a businessman as we were creating and implementing the vision.

The SENOs' leaders also indicated that they instill the same entrepreneurial mindset in all human resources in the organization. The participants shared that flourishing starts with the workforce attitude and desire to make the SENO flourish. To explain, one manager indicated that as a SENO, they need a very good competitive recruitment process to make sure that they recruit the right people into the right positions with the right mindset. Titus further commented, "You need individuals with entrepreneurial skills because the approach in the enterprise sector is way different from the nonprofit. We need people who are creative and innovative if we are to be successful." Discussing the importance of a strong entrepreneurial workforce, Luke contended that they had almost closed the organization because they failed to recruit the right personnel. The Director remarked that the top leaders never had an experience in running a combined mission organization. As a result, the company suffered huge losses because they lacked knowledge on the business side, which in turn affected the revenue of the charity. He said that because of this, they operated in deficit for some years. They were literally operating a bankrupt organization. Luckily things changed in the SENO when the right people took over management of the organization.

The founders also discussed the need for mentoring and coaching for SENO executives to have a better perspective on running dual-mission organizations. Business coaching has been regarded as one element that helps SENOs to be more successful as a business as well as a charity organization. Kelvin of CYON said that, as an Executive Director of a nonprofit entity, he needed to know better how to run a social enterprising organization when venturing into hybrid organizations. After several years of struggling to be successful, he indicated that they engaged mentors who worked with leadership in operating the dual-mission entity. He remarked that this helped them develop a different entrepreneurial mindset. They became more creative and innovative through mentoring, helping top leaders to develop cognitive behaviors that oriented toward opportunity recognition and value creation in context.

Running SENOs calls for leaders oriented to seeing opportunity and responding to that opportunity. These are cognitive thinkers—the ability to be imaginative and perceive and plan for the operation of the organization. Cognitive thinkers are more innovative and creative in their work. For instance, The Art Box Ltd. is able to see potential in using waste to creating craft that they are able to sell to the upper-end market. They make crafts from used plastics, toothpaste tubes, pasta packets, and much more. Leaders display good cognitive industrial understanding in their thinking. Literature like Bekki et al. informs that an entrepreneurial mindset plays a pivotal role in creating opportunities. The long-term survival and flourishing of organizations, like The Art Box Ltd. and others, rests on how industrial they are in their activities. For the SENO, the entrepreneurial mindset behavior is crucial to the long-term success of the organization because it helps the leaders to be more innovative and creative, especially in regard to managing change and uncertainty.

5.2.1 Managing Change in SENO

Study participants remarked that SENOs operate in a constantly changing and turbulent environment. This change is influenced by the economic, political, technological, and natural phenomena of the country. Successful SENOs are therefore capable of change management. Several participants believed that organizations that fail to incorporate change management strategies in their operation quickly fall into difficulties or liquidation. The founders of SENOs suggested that proper management of change is essential in the management of dual bottom-line organizations. Others explained that flourishing organizations understand the dynamics of adjusting and adapting to any environment in their operations. The Principal of RMM remarked:

> We need to understand the environment where we are working. For instance, there are several changes that are happening in the education sector in Malawi. As a school, when the national curriculum changes, we need to quickly adapt to that by training our teachers and buying new teaching and learning resources. There is a danger that our students can fail to perform well in national examinations when we fail to adapt to these changes. The failure of our students in national examinations means that we cannot attract new students to our school and some students may even leave us.

Indeed, understanding and adapting to change is central to operating in the uncertain environment for the organizations. SENOs quick to adapt are in a better position to outperform their competitors. This is the argument made by Madni, who called for companies to reevaluate their competitive positions by initiating change programs to assure long-term viability and competitiveness. Survival rests in the capability of the SENOs to adapt to changes in their operating environment. One founder indicated that their capability to manage change helps them to implement their objectives smoothly and thoroughly, even when conditions are not conducive.

The Malawi economy has been unstable for several years. A poor economy coupled with political instability for the past 2 or 3 years has rendered the business environment unfavorable to both local and international investors. Several organizations are scaling down or closing because of heavy taxation and corruption affecting the economy. The findings of this study suggest that managers must wisely invest and prudently manage their investments in an ever-changing economic and political landscape. The research participants highlighted the fact that the market fluctuates every day, so they need to modify the way they do their activities. Linda of Hope Inc. said:

> Sometimes it is difficult to find raw materials and when we get them, they are expensive due to the higher import tax imposed on goods. As an enterprise, we make sure that when we don't get the raw material we are looking for, we adjust to the reality and produce the best with what we have. That is why we suggest of purchasing our own machine that will enable us to make our own fabric. This will help us to control the raw material supply and we will not be directly affected by the economic changes in one way or another.

Adaptation to economic changes has not been easy for many dual-mission organizations in Africa. One participant explained that they almost closed the organization because they were losing much money due to the instability of the local currency, since they import most of their raw materials. He indicated that they are making profits now because they focus on using more locally produced raw materials. Their ability to adjust to new realities in the raw material industry has helped them meet challenges.

It was also observed that most SENOs in this study deliberately plan for change. The feeling among many founders is that the organizations that anticipate change in their industry and those that plan their operations remain relevant in the market. In addition, strategic planning has been one of the tools SENOs are using as a technique to adapt to change. The strategic plan gives the organizations a blueprint for their work and helps create alternative actions when the environment changes. The strategic plan helps organizations conduct environmental scanning, which helps them make anticipated changes in their industry. Furthermore, it was indicated that strategic planning helps the SENOs to deliberately control the market rather than respond to issues within their industry. Willie said that in YCON, they constantly meet to analyze the environment to help them anticipate challenges and opportunities in their industry.

Most founders explained that proper change management systems help in managing change, since the workforce is prepared for environmental risks and uncertainties. They believed that management structures help in employees' attitude and behavior toward change. The employees' positive attitude in the organization is important since it promotes individual citizenship behavior in the organization even in times of change. The competitive landscape is ever-changing in every industry in Malawi, which means the SENOs need to have a motivated workforce with the right attitude to remain relevant. Economic conditions, labor markets, and customer preferences all affect how business is conducted by the indigenous SENOs. This is echoed by Haas (2019) who shared that businesses need to understand the environment in order to meet stakeholders' needs, which will help in their success. He further believes that employees matter in this changing environment. SENOs that are surviving and performing well have a proper change management system built within the workforce. Kotter (1988) contends that effective change management is critical to success of any organization. He developed eight steps of change management. In his eight steps for change, he pointed out that a sense of urgency for change is essential for successful change management.

Successful SENOs strive to create a change-embracing culture within the system that is ethical at the same time. In ethical culture, participants called for ethical change implementation built into the integrity of the institution. Successful SENO leaders inspire and champion positive change by providing information to employees. For instance, Kelvin of CYON remarked that they communicate honestly and transparently about any change in the operation of his organization. In doing so, the organization creates a policy statement that binds the workforce to a set of values and ethical standards.

5.2.2 *Managing Risk and Uncertainty*

The interview findings further indicated that taking risks is the fundamental nature of running an organization in Malawi. Research findings reveal that risk is inevitable in running any entrepreneurial organization, whether profit-oriented or nonprofit. The environment provides several challenges to the flourishing of the entity. Findings suggest that risks influence the quality of the products/services, growth of the organization, and profitability of the SENO. The interviewees explained that clear risk management systems help SENOs in their quest for flourishing. For instance, leaders in many SENOs take proactive measures to overcome uncertainties that will protect the resources and assets of the entity. The SENOs in this study create a culture that is able to anticipate and innovatively mitigate the risk. The study participants maintained that establishing a strong risk culture to proactively deal with risk is essential to success. Since they faced competition from products that were unbranded but cheaper from other artisans, Hope Inc. intensified its online shopping efforts because this was the only market that had remained untapped by the artisans selling unbranded products. The SENO developed a risk resilience approach to thriving in their environments. The approaches are consistent with many SENOs and help in the flourishing of the enterprises. Gatzert et al. (2015) contended that developing enterprise risk management programs enables organizations to manage corporate risk in a holistic way rather than the silo-based approach.

To mitigate risk, several SENOs ran multiple businesses either to increase revenue for charity or to mitigate the loss when one enterprise fails. This risk management strategy was talked about by several founders. Bill explained that they have seven enterprises that run independently of each other. He remarked that, as a SENO, "We don't want to put all our eggs in one basket." Notably, the idea behind running multiple businesses is that these enterprises can help each other when needed. For instance, CAISD indicated that they use the profits from one company to help the other company stand on its own. Relying on one company can be risky to the long-term success of the organization. These sentiments were also shared by the programs coordinator of Hope Inc., who said that they want to make the refugee camp a center of activity in the city to run several business ventures. She remarked, "We are planning to open a food court and organize several cultural events that will attract people at a fee … this will help us to diversify into other business ventures which will help us to raise more funds for our charity work." The approach of running multiple businesses has been practiced by almost all SENOs. One SENO has seven enterprises with different management systems. They know that when the market for one business is not conducive, they will be compensated by the other business. This results in revenue from the businesses throughout the year.

In addition, SENOs focus on the capability of the organization in both business and social activities. The SENOs choose to invest in an industry in which they have the knowledge and the capabilities to succeed. One SENO indicated that they are into education because the founders have a vast experience in running educational institutions. At the same time, another SENO mentioned that they closed a college because none of the directors knew how to run such an educational institution. Many managers interviewed seem to believe that having individuals with the right skills, abilities, and knowledge helped them proactively deal with risk and uncertainty. At the same time, when risk comes, they are able to control the impact of the risk on the organization. Therefore, the importance of managing risk cannot be overemphasized for SENOs. It has been noted also that the ability to manage risks increases stakeholder confidence. Successful risk management in the organization provides stability in the organization. This is possible when an organization has well-qualified employees; recruiting and training them is the role of human resource units of organizations.

5.3 Chapter Conclusion

Operations management of the SENOs has been one of the crucial issues raised by leaders of the SENOs. The study uncovered that SENO leaders who are running social enterprises find it hard to succeed on the market. The participants indicate that managing the day-to-day operations of the entity becomes an important aspect in the flourishing of the SENO. Management is regarded as the business function that focuses on managing the day-to-day process of creating services and goods. It helps in building the operation capabilities of the enterprise that allow the company to create value for customers and other stakeholder in the production process.

Chapter 6
Human Resource Management

The management of human capital plays an integral role in the flourishing of SENOs. Human resource management involves attracting, developing, rewarding, and retaining employees for the benefit of both the employees as individuals and the organization as a whole. The study participants indicated that HR departments interact with other departments to make sure that qualified people for the positions that exist in the organization are recruited and properly oriented and trained. As a result, the goals of human resources in these organizations reflect and support the goals of the rest of the organization. Many founders explained that human resource management utilizes talents and opportunities within and outside their organization to create a stronger and more effective organization. According to several managers in this study, this involves the development of a consistent, aligned collection of practices, programs, and policies to facilitate achievement of the organization's strategic objectives. The findings show that the integration of all HR programs within a larger framework facilitates achievement of goals, placing people at the center of strategic advantage of the organization. Flourishing of the SENO is closely linked to how an organization finds, treats, and manages its human capital.

SENOs that make people the center of competitive advantage are able to survive and flourish. Human resource management for SENOs must respond to the double bottom-line nature of the organizations. SENOs thus engage in dual alignment of human resources, that is, ensuring that the charity and business sides of SENOs have appropriate personnel that ensure the achievement of goals. This dual alignment of human capital must attend to both positions in the organizations vertically across the hierarchy of the organization but also horizontally, that is, positions across similar ranks. The following discussion addresses six human resources elements that drive indigenous SENOs into flourishing.

Z. Chijere, *Nonprofit Social Enterprises*, CSR, Sustainability, Ethics & Governance, https://doi.org/10.1007/978-3-031-60234-4_6

6.1 Recruiting Right Employees

The success of any SENO is built on individuals working in the organization. The founders of flourishing SENOs explained that, to a large extent, the performance of the organization depends on the quality of the individuals within it. Mike of CAISD stressed the significance of building a team that drives the organization toward success. He said:

> Make sure you have got that team around you…, find the right people to work for the organization. Then use the people and use the talents that you have to the best of the organization. The organizations should strive to get the individuals that are well equipped and prepared to do the work. Find people that have the right skills and knowledge to do the job. If you have this, you are assured of success even in tough economic environments.

Kelvin, the founder of CYON, similarly pointed out that he "would rather hire well-qualified staff in the first place, because as a private institution we need a strong team of teaching staff in order to attract more students." He added, "But for us we said we would be recruiting well qualified teachers who will provide the quality education, and that aspect has helped us also to be where we are now." The importance of having and managing talents was observed in several flourishing SENOs. In agreement, Bruce, Hope Inc. Executive Director explained:

> Now, coming into this resource which is the most important resource it took a bit of time to realize the importance and then with time we said no, I think we need to put much effort here, we need to make sure that we have got good policies, we need to make sure that there is very good care given to this group of people to this resource and then also how do we make sure that this resource is contributing positively to the growth of the organization.

In order to attract and keep talent, human resources strategic planning is a crucial component for any SENO's mission. Organizations with a clear strategy to attract talent are able to succeed. Human resources strategy guides the organization to what they can do and what they cannot do in the process of managing people. Finding talent that fits well into the organization is not easy for many SENOs, since they do not properly plan for human capital. While some find it easy, others find it difficult to find the right individuals who can work in the enterprise. Linda of Hope Inc. explained:

> I just see so much potential but then because I don't have a team of ten highly skilled people, I want to run but I can't. Anyway, we are already doing a lot and so if some of my staff were more experienced in accounting, for example, we would do more than that. But when you are a small enterprise, you cannot get those highly skilled because you cannot afford to pay their salaries, so it's a matter of time.

This amplifies the importance of having a clear HR strategy with a good recruitment process. There are several strategies that these SENOs use in order to find the right individuals. The first strategy is hiring close friends of the leadership team and expanding the workforce around these friendships. Most of these SENOs were founded by very close friends who had known each other for some time before they created the organization. The first group of friends acts as the executive board. Then, they recruit more through relationships and some through job application merit.

Thus, it is easy for them to keep on recruiting based on the connections they have in the industry. This gives the SENOs a competitive advantage regarding skills because they recruit individuals who already have strong bonds among them. This acts as fuel for success in their operation. For instance, CAISD was founded by four individuals who went to school together. These individuals are the core of the operations and at the same time are running different enterprises within CAISD. The story is similar to those of RMM and CYON, which were started by close friends who wanted to make a difference. This provided an opportunity for people with different skill sets to work toward success. This approach has the advantage that the team is able to stay together over the long term, which helps the continuity of the operations.

Several founders also shared that they deliberately train individuals who will come back and work for them. This is mostly in the form of scholarships both for existing staff to take up higher-level positions and for high school graduates who would later see the need to give back. This is a unique strategy that many SENOs use as a means of deliberately cultivating individuals who are willing to give back to the organization. A founder of MSAHI said that they send over a thousand young people to different high schools and colleges both inside and outside the country by offering scholarships every year as part of their charity work. The organization later employs some individuals from among the sponsored graduates. Some come back as interns, volunteers, or full-time staff. He reported that these graduates have strong connections with the organization, which makes it easier for them to deliver when they are employed. He explained:

> I have a program where I send students to different colleges across the globe, some even in the United States, China, and other countries. Some, of course, study in our own colleges in Malawi. So out of these, those whom I feel are good students, I invite them to help me since I have been giving them school fees, I feel they can also do good to others. Most of our top managers here are beneficiaries of this scholarship program. So, for us, we are never in short supply of well qualified individuals who can work with us.

This is the same with CSE deliberately employing individuals who have undergone formal training at one of their centers. Most of the staff were deliberately identified and trained with an aim of bringing them back as capacity-builders and even as creators of new enterprises for the organization. These individuals are later a good fit for the SENO because they already have strong links to the institution.

6.2 Managing the Needs of the Workforce

Finding talent alone is not enough; managing talent is also central to the success of the SENO. Several managers indicated that treating human capital with dignity results in happy living for the workforce, which in turn translates into happy living organizations. This resonates with previous studies such as Liu (2019) who argued that the way an organization treats its talent affects the success of its activities. He emphasized that humanistic aspects like good working conditions and good treatment influence employees' attitude toward work. The findings show that a satisfied workforce is motivated to work hard toward the achievement of goals and that well-treated staff are willing to stay long with the organization. So, the desire to leave the job is reduced when the workers feel respected and treated with dignity. Proper management of employment relations supports organization citizenship behavior among workers. It is clear that the way the organization sees value in the workforce contributes a lot toward the attitude and the performance of individuals on the job.

Empowerment is another strategy that several organizations in this study used to keep talent and attract more talent. The findings revealed that an empowered workforce contributes more to the success of the entity. Several managers explained that independence has been proven to be a great motivator for personnel in these organizations and is an important aspect of managing talents in SENOs. John, one of the top managers at CYON, explained how their company creates a staff-friendly environment by giving them independence in executing their duties:

> We have given a bit of independence to the individuals whilst, of course, they may need to refer to us in some cases but at least there is a sense of flexibility. We give them that mandate to flexibly propose ideas and suggestions. Then we endorse the ideas they are able to suggest, even others they will do without endorsing as long as they are making positive contribution to the company.

Thus, individual autonomy in the workplace is important in the success of the SENO. It allows workers to be innovative in their work, since they are able to think on their own to create success. The freedom and ability to work independently helps the workforce grow in creativity and feel enabled to drive the organization forward. Studies show that workplace autonomy further helps improve employee performance through increased creativity and innovation (Shier et al., 2019; Burde et al., 2017; James & Jones, 2013; Shanock et al., 2019). As indicated earlier, creativity and innovation are key elements in an entrepreneurial organization. Perceived organizational support of workforce freedom influences both employee morale and their retention rate. Therefore, the proper management of employees is central in keeping talent in the organization and helping those talents to perform beyond the expected levels and properly fit into the organization.

6.2.1 *Aligning Employees' Talents with Organizational Needs*

The proper alignment of employees with organizational needs is vital to the success of social enterprising nonprofit organizations. The ability to attract talents that are in turn placed in the right positions has been a central element in their success. Flourishing SENOs believe that employee skills, abilities, and knowledge of their work are keys to flourishing. For instance, the creative director for The Art Box Ltd., a Hope Inc. enterprise, explained that having the right people, especially artisans, in the right job is central in managing the organization. At the same time, she saw the need to fill positions with individuals who are qualified enough to do the work. Linda from Hope Inc. said:

> Finding the right individuals to do the work is key in our organization. However, we do not employ just any artisan; we look for those who are talented enough and who will fit into our vision and mission. We are affected both in the workforce morale and productivity the moment we bring wrong people in the enterprise.

This case echoes Liu (2019) in that perceived organizational support positively relates to behavior as well as to the psychological well-being of the workforce. The organizations realize that when the wrong people are placed in positions, they tend not to contribute their best to the institution. There is high staff turnover when there is a mismatch between the job and the individual. Brolis and Nyssens (2019) contended that a proper fit of individuals with organizations contributes positively to performance. There are high performance levels in the organization when individuals do what they are capable of doing.

The founders of several SENOs believed that good placement of individuals is a step toward a motivated workforce and a good organizational climate. When individuals are doing what they have been trained to do, their knowledge helps the organization to flourish. One founder explained about another failed entity within their SENO, saying, "There was a failure to properly see the need for the organization and the individuals who will fill the positions in the enterprise. We had people with zero knowledge about business running a multi-million-dollar entity."

Similar views were shared by another founder, who said that subsidiary companies are being managed by individuals who have the necessary knowledge and skills for what the enterprise is doing. The findings show that when qualified and skilled individuals are put in their right fields, it promotes effectiveness and leads to the success of the organization.

6.2.2 Managing Rewards and Compensation System

Many founders interviewed agreed that the compensation and reward system of the entity plays a role in boosting morale. A competitive reward system plays a big role in flourishing organizations. Working in a nonprofit sector is less rewarding in many indigenous organizations than working in for-profit enterprises; however, there is a changed mentality in flourishing SENOs. Flourishing dual-mission organizations focus on reward systems and making sure that employees are properly rewarded based on performance. The reward system includes a better salary scale (remuneration), better working conditions, and other extrinsic benefits that the employees receive based on the work they do. The positive pay practices contribute to staff commitment. In return, they believe that workers' attitude contributes positively to organizational citizenship, which in turn helps the performance of the organization.

Organizations that have better reward systems are successful in improving the morale of the workforce and in reducing individual intentions to leave the organization. For any extra amount of work that is done by the workforce, they receive an extra allowance that motivates them to cooperate when demand is high beyond normal hours. A workforce is motivated by rewards and benefits.

However, if the SENO cannot give them competitive salaries, they find something other than money to motivate them. Apart from giving them competitive salaries, the staff also benefit from the services/products of the SENO. Bill of CSE informed me that the children of their staff are part of the free education they give to the community. They receive complete support to keep the children either at their daycare center or primary school until their parents get off of work. This is the same with another SENO that allows two of the teachers' children or close relatives to attend school for free. This kind of reward helps the employees know that the organization cares for their welfare, which moves individuals to be dedicated to their work.

In general, compensation, rewards, incentives, and teamwork propel efficiency and effectiveness that helps institutions to flourish. Rewards and compensation systems are loosely linked with issues of justice. Jaristrom et al. (2018) argue that for sustainable human resource management, the organizations should focus on issues of fairness and equality in management. Also, the organizations should focus on meeting the legal and regulatory ecosystem within the labor industry for survival and creation of high-profile jobs. The ability to adhere to the legal framework within the labor market helps to manage issues for the SENO in a more ethical manner.

6.2.3 Employees' Organizational Commitment

The psychological commitment of individuals to SENO activities is one of the essential elements in human resource success. This psychological attachment can also be referred to as organizational citizenship behavior. Interviews with the founders revealed that the individual's organizational citizenship correlates with the performance of the firm as well as the performance of the whole workforce. The flourishing SENOs in this study work on instilling organization citizenship behavior in their employees at all levels. When talking about artisans' work, for instance, the Hope Inc. Creative Director remarked:

> There are times when our staff have a huge task to finish, and they have to work late. Their husbands do come with torches to get them when it is late. Sometimes they even take the machines home to do the work. In fact, we have many that are committed with that industrial kind of mindset.

The SENOs' desire to instill organizational citizenship behavior is consistent in most successful SENOs. The Station Manager for Y-Radio explained, "We need to have people at the cutting edge. People who are creative and dedicated. The employees' commitment to whatever we are doing is very important to our success." Many organizations focus on incentives in making people more committed to the organization. Many successful SENOs in this study focus on strategies that value their people. It is through the knowledge that they are valued that the workforce is able to have strong connections with the organization. The research participants further remarked that this strong connection helps employees feel that they are part of the organization. Liu et al. (2019) suggest that the value that the organization puts on the employees influences their attitude and behavior toward work. Their study further indicated that the incentive policies of an organization should focus on humanistic elements that promote individual attitudes. In addition, several study participants in this research see the need for transparency and accountability in leadership as helping to instill organization ownership in the employees. In this context, Titus of Tonga Foundation remarked:

> We have to make sure that people are comfortable. Transparency and accountability is key for sustainable institutions. People have to see that you are transparent on how you manage things because lack of transparency and accountability is one of the weaknesses attributed to most NGOs.

Titus indicated that for their institution, one thing they find very crucial is for the leadership to be upfront and straightforward with employees. He acknowledged that the success of an entity reflects the behavior of its staff. He remarked that the leadership attitude toward the staff is what dictates employee commitment or lack thereof. This means that things go well in the organization when staff are well motivated and have a sense of ownership of the entity. It is essential to instill a sense of ownership in the staff members. People should be able to point out where management and leadership are not doing well. The research participants indicated that management should also be able to accept criticism from the workforce. They say that leadership should value the views of the staff above the vision of the organization; it shows employees they are valued by the leadership.

6.3 Chapter Conclusion

Human resource management (HRM) plays an integral role for the flourishing of SENOs. This study has revealed that the flourishing of the SENOs is closely interlinked with the focus the enterprise puts on the people working for it. It is seen through this study that most SEs take people as the strategic competitive advantage that drives the organization to flourish. It is noted that the dual alignment of the HR in the vertical and horizontal system contributes to the performance of an organization. This chapter highlighted six human resource (HR) elements that drive SENOs.

Chapter 7
The Governance of a SENO

Governance is another integral element in the flourishing of social enterprising nonprofit organization. Governance refers to a process in which the authority influences and authorizes policies and decisions that will define the life of the organization and its conduct. The hybrid nature of the SENO calls for a governance approach that accommodates hybridity, addressing both business and charity needs. One of the founders mentioned that for any dual-mission organization to deliver development to people, the institution's governance system has to be strong on both ends. This means that one cannot run a successful SENO without proper governance that addresses the dual nature of the organization.

7.1 Upholding the Organizational Vision and Mission

Employees' mental image of the SENO plays an integral role in the success of the organization. This feeling was expressed by several founders who believe that the mission and vision of their organization is a blueprint for the institution's operations. They believe that having a clear mission motivates individuals to work toward accomplishment of its goals. Success rests in the clear mental blueprint that leaders have for the organization. The SENOs that were part of this study all indicated that they have a clear mission and operational compass that fuels their performance. The participants shared that a clear purpose provides a clear direction for the organization. The feeling among the founders was that the mission of the organization guides the SENO's position within the industry.

Vision is a joint effort created by the founders in consultation with the stakeholders. Luke of CDECO shared that they had spent over a month recreating their vision when they were expanding into the enterprising nature of the charity. He shared that they invited individuals who had been running successful social enterprising organizations across Africa to walk them through the vision creation process. They

Z. Chijere, *Nonprofit Social Enterprises*, CSR, Sustainability, Ethics & Governance, https://doi.org/10.1007/978-3-031-60234-4_7

deliberately got input from all necessary stakeholders when creating the vision and mission of the organization. The dual nature of the SENO calls for flexible missions and objectives that will accommodate both for-profit and nonprofit activities. This therefore calls for collaborative efforts among the important stakeholders in the organization.

Enterprises and nonprofits have two separate missions and objectives, which helps in creating their operational boundaries. The nature of SENOs facilitates the enterprises having for-profit mission and objectives as well as a social mission and objectives for charity. In this regard, social enterprises shift to more corporate governance, which is controlled by the board of directors, and the charity maintains its nonprofit governance nature, which is controlled by the board of trustees. For instance, CAISD indicated that in terms of mission and vision, they make sure that each company has a separate mission statement that is in line with the vision of the entity. In the same regard, the charity has a separate mission and vision that stirs the entity into performance. The organization knew that operating on one vision and mission for both charity and business could be cumbersome. Separating the two helps in managing the SENO within the limits of both operations.

Beyond simply creating the vision and mission, successful SENOs must operate within their mission. The SENOs indicated that their mission and objectives help them to adhere to and concentrate on the activities happening in the organization. The vision acts as a blueprint of their operations. As Kelvin of CYON indicated, "When you have a vision, take it all the way, until people understand, then you will succeed. Once the people understand it, they will appreciate it, but if you start changing and wavering, you will not go far." This means that the shared vision helps the organization to do what it is supposed to do. The goals set for the managers help the organizations to know what is expected of them. It gives them the direction in whatever they do because they know what the organization wants to achieve. Henry of CSE remarked that "the purpose of our work with the staff helps in maintaining our focus as an enterprise which guides us on how to use our resources and energy. It is the clear goals that drive our actions in the enterprise. It is through the mission that we are able to decide which businesses we can venture." It was widely accepted by all study participants that the mission instills a sense of ownership in the organization. The mission helps the workforce to know that the enterprise exists to help them to live a better life. It is indisputably clear from this study that having a clear mission and objectives helps with alignment within the organization.

7.1.1 Enhancing Quality of Products and Service

Maintaining the desired level and standard of quality for products or services is one of the elements of success raised by the study participants. In quality control, managers are faced with a decision to either correct problems immediately to get performance on track or to analyze the deviations and understand the causes of the quality variances. The findings suggest that managers utilize both of these strategies to ensure that the products/services are of highest quality. The ability to maintain product quality was highlighted as one issue in the survival and subsequent success of the organizations. Interviews with the founders indicated that producing products/services that meet the market specifications is an important element in success. Gilbert, a plant manager at MSAHI, said that they struggled in the first years of business as a SENO because the organization was making products without adhering to standards requirements. He said, "Currently the reports (coming out from the regulators) of the tests show that we are in the range of the required production (standards)." Concurring, a founder of another SENO explained: "We work to prevent any form of defects in what we are producing. We always brag that we are the best in the irrigation industry. We are in fact the market leaders because quality is our priority." The SENOs agree that the social enterprising nonprofit organizations that are doing well in the market focus on products that will meet the regulators' standards. The organizations understand that, beyond having charity status, they need to produce services/products that will be able to compete in the market.

In making sure that they have quality products and services, the SENOs shared that they strive to put in place systems that help them meet and maintain the standards in the products and/or services. Henry of MSAHI remarked that every industry that organizations venture into has regulations and product standard specifications. He believes that failure to comply with regulators' standards has a big impact on profitability. He said many times that organizations that fail to meet the regulators' standards face the danger of closure, and they had been in such situations in early years of their operations. Things didn't change until they saw the need of quality for their product. He believes that the standards are given, and the products are measured against the specifications. He says:

> If we fail to meet the specifications, the Bureau of Standards closes the production until we rectify the problem. This has an impact on the sales and the general operations of the company. I would say for the past three years we have been surpassing the product standards.

Process management is highlighted as an important element in assuring quality of products. Bill, a top manager at CSE, explained that process management entails the alignment of the production process to the desired standards set in the industry. He indicated that the SENOs establish measures by which they test the operation of the actual production to locate any misalignment with set standards. He further explained that inspection of the products has been a key strategy that the SENOs have been using to produce unique and high-quality products. They apply due diligence in making sure that what gets on the market goes through a thorough vetting process by the workforce. Noting the need for quality production and/or services, another manager highlighted the fact that quality in education is an excellent feature of their institution. William of RMM says:

> In the academic industry we make sure that the academic staff should be well qualified, students enrolled should be well disciplined, the curriculum material should be of high quality, the grading system should also be of high standard, the education should be conducive for both teachers and students. Quality is measured by its own standard set by the institution itself and checked and confirmed by external bodies such as the ministry of education. As you see this is a system that checks itself regularly.

The study reveals that quality assurance can often be different in service-oriented SENOs, as compared to those that are in production. This is the same argument by scholars such as Firzsimmons and Bordoloi (2014) who highlighted four aspects and qualities in service companies, of which two are relevant here: the simultaneous production and consumption and the tangibility of the services. The SENOs that are flourishing understand that even though they are in the service industry, they need to make sure that their services meet the required standards expected by both industry regulators and their customers. On top of that, they need to know that the service industry calls for due diligence in assuring quality, since there is no time to rectify any error in the service rendered to the customer. In this regard, the SENOs indicated the need to be cautious relating to and handling customers in business transactions.

Several service delivery SENOs spend money continuously to train their workforce to provide better services. On the tangibility aspect of the services, it is noted that the intangibility of the services makes them difficult to evaluate in advance. This argument is supported by several studies. Acuto (2010), for instance, pointed out that continuous quality improvement is essential to the success of any company. The SENOs focus on the planned, organized, and systematic process of ongoing, incremental, and company-wide changes in existing practices aimed at improving company performance. This calls for due diligence in making sure that what is being given to the customers is of high quality, because it is difficult to retrieve a service once it has been provided.

7.2 The Ownership Model of SENOs

The SENOs in this study pursued different ownership models. This impacted the design and approach to doing business and service. There are two major ownership models that were discovered in this study: the hybrid model and the single registration model.

The hybrid model involves dual registration of the organization. Following this model for Malawi, the nonprofit is incorporated within the registration requirements of the country, and the business entity is registered with the Registrar of Companies. Mike of CAISD said they include both the board of directors and the board of trustees in their approach. The business section becomes the Limited Company, while the nonprofit section gets Trustee status. He, however, said that the two coexist because one cannot be separated from the other. In this dual ownership model, the enterprise is registered as a separate entity to become a limited company. Therefore, the two entities have a separate management system and financial system. How does this impact the thriving of the organization? According to several SENOs, they separated their companies to increase chances of growth for individual entities because when they were operating the charity and the business as one, they noted that some entities were holding back the growth of others. This made it hard for the organizations to see whether they were making a profit. In such a case, there was no motivation for individual companies to move forward and grow. In general, the leaders separated the entities to ensure that they are able to monitor growth in the independent entities.

In the single registration model, the business part of SENO is not registered as a limited company but still has a separate arm and operates as a profit-making entity. In this approach, the enterprise gets certification within the industry; however, there is no separate company structure operating the enterprise. The approach follows a single management system and financial system that oversee the management of both the charity and the business activities. In this ownership model, most top decisions are made by the founder, at times together with the top management team, which can be full of self-interest. This means that growth and success take time to materialize. Most managers explained that in this approach, one needs a strong institution with a strong governance structure and a functioning board of trustees that controls the operations of the organization. The feeling among the founders is that it is easy to manipulate the entity when there is no board of trustees to control the profit-making and usage. Nevertheless, the majority of the SENOs sampled in this study take this ownership model.

7.2.1 Complying with the Product/Service Regulatory Standards

This study found that the quality of products and services is an important element in creating a sustainable and flourishing SENO. As highlighted earlier, several founders indicated that a highly reliable product comes out of high-quality process and a highly reliable manufacturing system. SENOs in this study realize the importance of high-quality production for the success of the organization. SENOs invest in machinery that will help produce high-quality goods and services. It is noted that conformity to the standards in the industry and producing high-quality products and services have been one of the essential matters discussed by managers and founders. Optimal design quality, conformance quality, and price decision are positively interrelated. Quality in a SENO is a multifaceted element that refers to many things such as non-inferiority or usefulness of a product/service. Operating within and even above the standards set within the industry is key to the flourishing of the entity. Remarking on how they comply with legal requirements in the product standards, Dave of MSAHI said:

> Some of the challenges we meet depend on the Malawi Bureau of Standards. Sometimes they find minor faults, which we easily and mostly address. Overall, we strive to work in a manner that meets the standards of MBS in our products. The production team follows a set of procedures that the company has put in place to produce quality products.

This argument resonates with several other SENOs. The findings reveal that the SENOs set a work framework that helps them to comply with the authorities. For instance, CAISD is also in the construction industry and works under the supervision of the National Industry Construction Council (NICC), their regulator. William of CAISD concurred with others when he pointed out that to run a school, one needs to operate within the requirements set by the government under the Ministry of Education Science and Technology (MoEST). He said: "We need proper facilities like classrooms, library, good bathrooms and a laboratory. As an institution, we have all that and we have gained trust from our community." The SENOs indicate that conformance promotes the performance of the entity, since conformance to standards helps the SENOs to produce products/services that are reliable and durable for the consumer.

An organization's strategic plan is an important aspect of the compliance process, especially in the production of durable and reliable products/services. The findings of this study indicated that in order to satisfy the customers' needs and maintain their loyalty, the organization needs to conform to the regulators' standards in their environment. If SENOs are to be successful, they should focus on producing products/services that conform to the regulators' standards. He et al. (2020) remarked that there is a natural relationship between quality and reliability. Several social enterprise managers focus on creating a system that promotes quality in the entire production process. Embracing an enterprise-wide strategy for quality assurance and regulatory compliance has helped many SENOs to build a culture that focuses on operating within the quality standards in their industry. The wide-range strategy in the standards conformance process helps to create competitive advantages for the company, since firms are able to produce superior products that match or even surpass the cost on the market. Findings from this study's observations reveal that the wide-range strategy calls for an organization's wide focus on the skill development of all the people involved. Such trainings facilitate the abilities of the workforce to focus on meeting regulatory standards. Henry explained at length how he makes sure that his production team regularly attends staff development training, which helps them to be in adherence with the regulator in their industry.

7.2.2 *Formulating and Implementation of the Strategic Plan*

The blueprint of the SENO operation is embedded in the strategic plan of the organization. This means that for SENOs, strategy is critical. The founders of SENOs shared that in the governance of the entity, strategic planning and making sure that the plan is implemented with precision have been a central concept in the success of the organizations. Several founders remarked that it is important to align the strategic planning process with business process management if the organizations are to be successful. This alignment helps the SENO to act in line with their mission and strategy. Findings from the interviews revealed that planning and organizing helps the enterprises not to drift from the vision and mission of the entity. For many SENOs, planning provides direction. Kelvin of CYON comments:

> It would be necessary to continue with the income generating part whilst maintaining the vision for the organization. In principle, the business is coming to support the social enterprise. I know that at some point in time, the businesses are more visible than the nonprofit. For us to avoid moving away from our original vision, we have maintained the NGO as the biggest part. We attribute the strategic planning and adhering to that strategy as one of the approaches that have helped us not to drift away from our mission.

The planning process in this organization, like many others, takes both formal and informal dimensions. The managers use any opportunity to create the direction for the institution. For CYON, planning helps them to be more proactive in the market than just reacting to the event and gives the SENOs an upper hand over their competitors in the industry.

Several other participants indicated that strategic planning helps to minimize redundancy and waste of resources in their enterprise. Proper planning keeps the managers in control of how to distribute scarce resources without waste. Phillip of CSE remarked, "I bring all my managers once a week to know what is happening in each department. We share our goals, needs and plans. This helps me as a leader to know how I can prioritize resource allocation." Lack of proper planning and organizing makes the leaders blindly spend on activities that are not relevant. Sometimes, leaders made poor investment decisions because of lack of a blueprint for their actions.

Proper planning, as indicated by another founder, helps in reducing uncertainties within their organization. William of CAISD said that since managers are custodians of an organization's direction, the creation of an operations blueprint helps them to understand the operations of their institutions and to know what to anticipate in the work environment. The ability to reduce or to shift risk has been an essential element in the success of SENOs. Proper planning and organizing strategies have helped the SENOs to flourish, even in uncertain business environments. At the same time, other participants indicate that it is easy to adapt to change and failure when the operations of the enterprise are properly planned.

7.2.3 Monitoring and Evaluation of the Dual Mission

Several managers interviewed indicated that monitoring and evaluation (M&E) is one of the elements that help in the governance of SENOs in Malawi. Continuous monitoring and evaluation provide an avenue to assess the progress a SENO is making. The SENOs that are doing well put their efforts into evaluating the performance of their entities. This helps them in better planning and implementing their strategies. Bill of CSE emphasized the importance of M&E in his enterprise. He explains that they make sure they have weekly management meetings to evaluate the progress of each enterprise, and this helps them figure out how they can keep improving their business. Analysis showed that evaluation helps managers to examine the effectiveness, relevance, efficiency, and impact of the firm's activities. One founder remarked that M&E helps managers in the organization to isolate errors and defects in the products before they get on the market. He said that they use constant meetings that help them evaluate the business as the activities are happening. When they find themselves in an awkward environment, they normally meet and review their work. They meet as directors, checking and analyzing how they are performing in different departments, both in the charity and business sections of the organization. He explained that the feedback process within the organization is important in the management of the SENO. The meetings help them to gather the important feedback they need in the governance of the organization. Study participants indicated that when they monitor and evaluate activities in their organizations, they make sure that the workforce understands expected performance and that the staff are involved in the process. In this, the SENOs focus on giving relevant feedback to personnel. Mike (CAISD) explained:

> We do ensure that we are providing a platform through which staff at all levels are able to provide feedback and that is done through promoting and encouraging meetings in the departments. We also have an open office policy in the organization. Anyone regardless of position can come to me or other directors to share their concern. As a leader, I'm always ready to tell my staff what is happening in the organization. As a company, we are able to get feedback, on how we are all doing.

As indicated by this founder, good planning combined with effective M&E enhances effectiveness and success for the SENO by promoting employees' confidence in their work. Noting the same, Urban discussed the fact that continuous assessment promotes self-efficacy in implementing the vision. Self-efficacy, according to Bandura (1994), is the belief in one's life ability to influence events in one's life and to control how these events are experienced. This is the capacity to develop execution behavior necessary to produce performance attainment. Findings in this study show that M&E combined with self-efficacy promotes sustainability, innovativeness, and financial returns for the enterprises. This is because the M&E process helps the SENO learn from the past in order to repeat or avoid some actions that are associated with the performance of the enterprise.

7.3 Establishing Organizational Policies for Operations

Organizational policy emerges as one of the governance issues that have an influence on the operation of an enterprise. Findings from the interviews show that flourishing SENOs put in place guidelines and best practices within its operation. Several founders indicated that they have a clear guideline on employee practices, a code of conduct, disciplinary procedures, and other manuals that guide the behavior of the SENOs and the individuals working under them. One founder specifically said that every social enterprising nonprofit organization needs to have clear policies that define behaviors within the company. The founders argued that having no policies makes it difficult to control the behavior of the people, which will lead the organization into chaos. This is echoed by several managers who shared that, in their enterprise, policies are put in place to ensure that whatever one is doing is of excellence.

As an organization, they have written documents that dictate how each individual working with the organization should behave and adhere to their work standards.

The intriguing question is why the SENOs focus on creating guidelines and policies in their governance. Findings indicated three major reasons. First, they indicated that the policies help to protect the image of the enterprise. As Bruce of Tonga Foundation remarked, “We all need to work under some framework that will protect the image of the organization.” With clear guidelines, no one can complain of favoritism or unethical conduct because the required behavior is written out in the organization’s manuals. The findings suggest that the policies are key in establishing boundaries on behavior of the managers and other workers. The guidelines give the managers a direction as to what good behavior is. Standardized guidelines help give boundaries to all individuals on what they can or cannot do while working. Policies help everyone to know what is required of each individual in the organization, and they provide consistency in standards. Second, findings revealed that SENOs with clear policies create a conducive work environment for their employees. Many managers interviewed shared their belief that knowing the code of conduct and other procedures within the company creates a good working atmosphere. This kind of knowledge creates a trusting environment because everyone knows that work and conduct are transparent. This helps the SENOs create a trusting and well-regulated environment that promotes organizational citizenship behavior in the workforce. The policy provides the framework of acceptable conduct which, if adhered to by the employees, fosters an innovative environment that helps SENOs to stand out in the market. Though not directly linked with profitability, these policies help the SENOs to create a system that promotes behaviors that contribute to the profitability of the firm, behaviors including worker commitment, staff retention, diverse work environment, and innovative behaviors.

7.4 Chapter Conclusion

SENOs’ governance has been regarded as important aspects of organizational flourishing. These are the first three elements that build the capabilities of the internal system of the organization. The dual bottom-line nature of a SENO calls for a deliberate approach in designing the organization and building the human capital of the institution. Several research participants, point out that the flourishing of a blended value organization depends on how it manages the dual bottom-line aspects of the organization. The goal is to create independent but coexistent charity and social enterprising arms of the organizations. The success in creating this coexistence has been one driving force for the flourishing of several SENOs in this study.

Chapter 8
Leadership in SENO

Leadership is a critical factor in the flourishing of social enterprising nonprofit organizations (SENOs). Leadership is the influence that individuals or a team has in achieving the goal of an organization; it helps in creating the values and beliefs that drive behavior in organizations.

8.1 Organizational Leadership

The founders and top managers of the SENOs indicated that leadership is an important factor in the success of organizations. Leadership is regarded as the process of influencing others to understand and concur to the needs and vision of the leader to goal achievement. It further acts as a process of facilitating individual and collective efforts to accomplish shared objectives. Therefore, leadership is an influence on the followers and a process of goal achievement. Although the styles and approaches of leadership may differ, the participants interviewed for this study agreed that success rests with the leader and that person's approach to influencing individuals to achieve an organization's vision and mission. The research participants constantly shared their views that organizational success or failure rests with the leadership. Therefore, it is quite difficult to see organizational growth if the leadership does not have a clear vision on what is supposed to be followed. The interviews indicate that growth is closely linked to how the leaders align the leadership of the organization to strategically achieve the goals of the organization. Several leadership aspects were raised by the research participants in this study. These aspects include developing strategic leadership, adopting leadership style, developing emerging leaders, building a leadership succession plan, upholding leadership trust and credibility, and creating a diverse leadership team.

Z. Chijere, *Nonprofit Social Enterprises*, CSR, Sustainability, Ethics & Governance, https://doi.org/10.1007/978-3-031-60234-4_8

8.1.1 The Need for Strategic Leadership

The study uncovers that strategic leadership appears to be one of the key attributes of leadership for a successful SENO. The findings indicated that strategic leadership involves a deep level of analytical thinking and strategic implementation of activities in leading organizations. Strategic leadership, therefore, is the ability of a leader to express their strategic vision and motivate and persuade followers to achieve the goal. Strategic leadership involves strategic control and evaluation of the operation of an institution. It is noted in this study that strategic control and evaluation has a direct and total influence on the effectiveness of an organization.

Several founders shared their views that strategy makes a SENO effective. Leaders draw on strategy to formulate specific actions the organization needs to engage in. Changing an organization's strategy into action requires strong strategic leaders. This involves forward thinking. This is the ability to plan for the future rather than focusing much on the present. As the participants indicated, this calls for leaders with strong conviction about their vision and mission. The interview data revealed that this form of leadership calls for individuals who have the ability to think ahead and predict the future operational environment. The participants shared their belief that strategic leadership is a core component of establishing balanced organizational control, developing human capital, and identifying strategic intent for the present and future operation of the institution. This strategic intent helps the organization to plan for the future operations of the entity. Thinking strategically helps in inspiring the workforce to move beyond the day-to-day operations to future operations. In fact, participants reported that leadership has been pivotal in maintaining the forward focus of their organization and its workforce. Titus of Tonga Foundation indicated that forward thinking helps in making the dual-mission organization more productive and successful in its goal attainment since they anticipate the future. In the same regard, Peter of Care Malawi indicated that there is direct relationship between strategic leadership and the management capacity of the organization in goal attainment. This is because the organization is proactive in anticipating what the environment may bring in the operation of the entity.

Strategic leadership starts when leaders create right networks that help them to be critical of events in their industry. The founders believed that networks both inside and outside the organization become a technique for their ability to think. In addition, findings further revealed that strategic thinking does not happen in a vacuum; leaders need a good support system that will stimulate their thinking. This means that leadership's ability to create networks and interact with others in the industry guides the direction and success of the organizations. William of RMM said, "We make sure that we interact with others in the industry to understand their approach in running a school. We joined a network of private education institutions that helps us to be more innovative." RMM operates in a network of seven local schools and also joined a national network of private schools. This helps the leadership to understand the changes in the education sector while also being able to access several resources from the partners, and this has helped in the growth of the institution.

The observations and the document analysis show that a strong board of trustees helps the leadership in the thinking process and in being strategic in the activities of the entity. The institutions shared that the board of trustees is pivotal in strategic leadership of their organizations. Several founders felt that any SENO needs a strong board of trustees that will help in creating the vision and implementation of the strategies of the institution. They noted that a strong board of trustees creates and checks the strategic operations of the organization. The feeling among the founders was that it is easy for the organizations to fail in their mandate if they do not have a strong board of trustees. They shared that leaders need to have a system that will stimulate thinking on the creation and implementation of strategies. They regard the board of trustees and/or the board of governors as one of the most important governance structures that help organizations to be innovative and strategic and remain on track. They believe their leadership boards have been instrumental in driving the leaders to be critical in their leadership process.

There are several benefits of being a strategic SENO leader. Strategic leadership helps to develop an environment in which employees are forward focused. The study indicates that when leaders are strategic, it trickles down to help the entire organization to be futuristic in thinking. Instead of just focusing on day-to-day operations, the workforce is able to think about how to sustain the operations of the entity over the long term. Levi of Tonga Foundation shared how their strategic approach to leadership has helped the workforce to think ahead of time in their action, saying:

> I let the people feel that they too own the organization. This creates an innovative environment where the employees strive to give the best to the company. Our managers don't just focus on today's operations, they are able to propose and even implement strategies that have helped us to remain in business and grow.

Another founder echoed the statements, saying:

> All the directors in the organization are open minded, we are thinkers. This is the same kind of approach that all managers have taken in the operation of individual companies. They are critical when it comes to the operation of the organization in order to align the operations with the strategies.

Leaders are constantly working in an environment that is not stable because of the ever-changing nature of the business world. This calls for leaders and organizations to constantly recreate the way they do business. Strategic leadership helps their organizations to navigate in the turbulent operating environment successfully by constantly reevaluating their operations in the environment. Constant reevaluation helps the organizations to find innovative ways to implement their strategies. This resonates with several authors like Dinwoodie (2014), who posited that leadership is a crucial factor in creating an environment where the workforce is able to creatively think of approaches that will promote critical thinking in overcoming challenges in the environment. Leaders who are not strategic easily cripple the operations of the organization since they cannot navigate the unsteady working environment. In addition, strategic leadership aids workers in decision-making. It is understood that strategic leadership contributes to the productivity of the organization, since it helps leaders to critically analyze the environment before they venture into any decision. Strategic leadership and thinking helps the firm to focus on the environmental variables of success in their decision-making, which increases the productivity of the entity (Mintzberg, 1978). The majority of the success rests on the leaders' ability to analyze the environment before making important decisions. Mike of CAISD explained it as follows:

> I would say that it really makes a great contribution, approximately over 60%, actually even more because the direction of the organization depends on the leadership. It is the leadership that gives actual direction where we are going and how we should get there and it is the leadership that provides the motivation even to the staff to make sure that they are well motivated and able to make positive contributions to achieving the objectives of the organization.

Furthermore, strategic leadership promotes data-based decision-making, which helps in aligning operations with the objectives of the organization. Levi shared that the ability to make decisions based on data drives the organization into creativity and innovation because the decisions are made based on real issues happening in the organization. For many participants in this study, decision-making is one of the central tenets in leadership; they believe that strategic leadership promotes data-based decisions, which leads to the success of their organization. This is echoed by Bunzli, who posited that strategic leadership has the ability to create a mental fictionization, making the flexibility and continuous thinking in the management of the entity. The mental ability and continuous thinking of the leader are important to the long-term success of any social enterprising organization. It helps in the creation of strategies that contribute to effective and efficient operations of the organization.

8.1.2 Leadership Styles in SENO

The question that keeps arising is "What types of leadership is used by a flourishing SENO?" Leadership approaches and styles are essential in inspiring success for any form of organization. How the leaders carry out their leadership has been regarded as an especially important element in the leadership success of a SENO. There are several leadership styles that were highlighted by the participants of this study. Three were dominant as being the leadership styles that most flourishing SENOs adopt. The leadership styles that were highlighted were team leadership, participative leadership, and servant leadership.

First, team leadership was found to be essential in the operation of each leader's SENO. They shared that the root of their organizations' success is the team approach in which the leadership creates a well-coordinated workforce. The organizations focus on deliberately creating a well-balanced team within the activities of the organization. Leaders in this leadership style strongly believe that it takes a group effort in a collaborative manner to easily achieve the organizational objectives. Team leadership increases collaboration while decreasing competition among the staff in the SENOs. William of RMM remarked:

> I believe so much in cooperation. I have made the people under my watch to know that the performance of the company is based on how each one has played their part. They know we work as a team, which means the more coordinated we are, the more successful we become. We build that spirit in the staff, we depend on each other, and we support each other for better performance.

Many founders interviewed seemed to suggest that there is a potential distraction to the operation of the SENO that comes when there is unhealthy competition in the organization. Therefore, SENO leaders find that team leadership helps the staff to see each other as associates, not competitors.

The second type of leadership that emerged from the interviews is that of participative leadership. Participative leadership is a kind of leadership in which the staff gives input on most decisions in the organization. Leaders using this style deliberately involve their staff in making strategic decisions in the organization. Several founders shared that they utilize various meetings with the top leadership to evaluate the organization's performance and give feedback on operations. They reported that most decisions are made only after thorough consultation with the management team, which helps them to gather diverse opinions before making a decision. One participant said that they focus on the participatory nature, since it helps the acceptability of the firm's decisions and business approaches. Phillip of CYON remarked, "The station focuses on involving the audience in the way the programs are designed. So, several programs we air on the radio are as a result of consultations we have had with several stakeholders." The participatory approach of leadership encourages creative solutions by bringing in a variety of opinions to the table in the organization. The study also revealed that the participatory nature helps to improve the morale of the workforce, since they know they are liable for the outcomes of their operation.

The last leadership style that was highlighted by the participants is that of servant leadership. Servant leadership is the understanding that the leader is a servant first. It begins with the natural feeling that one wants to serve first (Greenleaf, 1970). This mirrors the philosophy of Lao Tzuin (600 BC) who wrote that the greatest leader forgets himself and attends to the development of others. This is the concept of servanthood in leadership. The flourishing SENO leaders explained that servant leadership helps them to build a strong organization that facilitates the performance of the enterprise because the leaders are able to rise above self-serving desires to focus on promoting the welfare of the staff. Bruce remarked:

> We have taken servant leadership. We thought if we appear to them as servants, we work with them together so that we don't seem to be leading but that together, we create a platform for us all. We can call it leading from behind, so that at the end of the day, they will not say we have been led.

For the SENO, the needs of the staff are central, and the SENO seeks to build its strategic advantage on motivated staff. Rather than taking full control, leaders in the SENOs seek to serve others, which includes customers, staff, and other stakeholders.

8.2 Developing the Emerging Leaders in the Organization

The SENO that is flourishing gives the entire workforce a chance to learn and grow in their respective responsibilities. The findings revealed that in the flourishing SENO, leadership development mostly focuses on helping the workforce to gain both tacit and explicit knowledge through formal and informal training. The founders interviewed affirmed that leadership development has been key to the development of personnel in most social enterprising organizations. The observations of successful organizations show that the training process begins with some type of triggering event, both in the internal and external structure of the organization. A triggering event occurs when the manager recognizes that actual organizational performance is less than the expected performance. It is this triggering event that informs the leaders or the managers of the need to help the workforce to get some form of skills or knowledge in their operation. The managers remarked that these triggering events range from individual staff failure to meet targets to the general failure of the organization in meeting its targets.

The research participants reiterated that improving current or future work performance by imparting knowledge, changing attitudes, or increasing skills is essential to the success of the organization. The ultimate aim of leadership development is to enhance the current and future performance of the organization itself by developing the current and future staff. In this, the leaders focus on helping the workforce in gaining knowledge, skills, and attitudes that will improve the performance of both the individual and the organization they are serving. There are four strategies that the SENOs use to develop leaders for the organization.

First, the organizations deliberately invest in formal education by sending people to colleges through the charity organization. The idea is to raise new generations of leaders who will come back and take different responsibilities in the SENO. One of the successful organizations to adopt this approach is MSAHI. The founder has a program that sends people from the organization and recent high school graduates to different training institutions. For several years, they have been deliberately identifying future staff from these beneficiaries. This is one of the unique natures of the flourishing dual-mission organization. They take a deliberate role in creating a scholarship program for the communities they serve. They are able to identify talent through these scholarships. The SENOs who adopt this approach do not have to struggle to fill vacant positions in the organizations.

Second, several founders indicated that they delegate most of the responsibilities to staff as a means of training them to take up more challenging responsibilities. Findings reveal that delegation has been key in developing leaders for the successful organizations in this study. Respondents shared the importance of delegation in the process of developing and raising new leaders. Several research participants explained that through delegation, they learn which individuals are capable of managing different activities in the organization. Many founders reported that they are able to promote individuals into different positions based on how they perform when they are given tasks and responsibilities. Maggie of RMM reported:

> I do try as much as possible to instill the same leadership in my employees by making sure that those that I trust with some leadership responsibilities are given a room to fly on their own as they discharge their responsibilities. In case they make a mistake, that's a welcome development for me, because through those mistakes, they learn and grow. I therefore, make sure that when I delegate responsibilities, I am not stepping in their footsteps again but let them fly on their own.

This shows that through delegation, leaders are able to train and coach emerging leaders as they carry out their jobs. In addition, leaders are able to employ several monitoring approaches that help them to mentor more leaders in the organization through the delegation process. Delegation helps the organizations to give the workforce an opportunity to observe work in progress. SENOs use on-the-job training and understudy programs within the organization to train their workforce in various skills, abilities, and knowledge about their job.

8.3 Building Leadership Succession Systems

Leaders do not last forever. Succession is inevitable in a firm's life cycle. The SENO that is flourishing realizes that succession is not a one-time activity. Interviews indicated that a succession plan has been crucial in the success of the enterprising nonprofit organizations. In this study, succession refers to the process through which an organization plans for and fills senior level openings in the organization. The findings from the founders show that they deliberately have a clear succession plan in their strategy for the continuation of the organization; Mike shared that the survival and subsequent success of their organizations depend on the succession plan that is set in place. The findings also show that the SENO that is doing well has a good plan in place to facilitate the continuity of the organization after the founder and even the top leader have gone. The long-term continuity of the institution is one of the distinguishing marks of those institutions that are doing well as compared to those that are struggling.

Interview findings show that successful organizations focus on both the external and internal environments of the organization. The findings in this study show that very few managers from outside the organization implement change as compared to those from the inside. Several founders felt that the failure rate is high with external executives due to high board expectations set when hiring them. Several managers have shown that selecting executives through internal recruitment is ideal, which is in agreement with the founders. The managers believe that those from within the entity have more knowledge about the entity and will increase its productivity and chances of success. For this, the organizations utilize the internal promotions in filling top positions. Kelvin, the founder of CYON, described it this way:

> So, we have to instill responsibility in the people that we work with. We have to believe in our human capital. Everyone who is here has the leadership ability and can lead. I cannot stay for another two years. I have to go.

There are several strategies of succession that SENOs use. No matter the approach, how the successors are identified and developed is integral in these dual-mission organizations. The first of these approaches is the natural succession process. Some of the organizations in this study have natural successors waiting in the organization. The organizations are closely identified with the founder or the top leadership. Thus, these organizations take on the personal identity of the founder, as it is hard to separate the founder from the institution. In other instances, the SENOs have more than one founder, which helps the enterprises to be clear on who will fill in different major positions in the entity. For instance, CAISD uses a rotating executive directorship. Mike, CAISD's current director, explained how the rotation goes: I have been serving as the Executive Director because what we do on executive directorships is that we give each other terms. Four of us rotate and serve for 2 years and another will take over after that.

He continued, explaining that this rotation gives an opportunity for diversity because each person brings their skills to the table in terms of how they run the affairs of the organization, and by the end of the day, it helps the company in terms of diversity instead of just having one person being at the helm of the organization. He says:

> So that's actually the major benefit to the organization and apart from that, we as an organization learn, because when I am given the mantle to run as the Managing Director, definitely I have to rise up to handle most of the pressures around and whilst that is happening, I am learning.

The natural succession approach helps to ensure that the key positions are filled by individuals who have a history with the organization. The key positions are occupied by the individuals who not only have the right skills, capabilities, and experience but who also are already connected with the organization.

The second approach that the organizations utilize is voluntary succession within the organization: the owners decide who takes over after they leave. In this strategy, the founders have more power to dictate the succession process of the organization. It is regarded as one of the most convenient approaches that the SENOs are using. The founder in the voluntary succession approach grooms someone. That someone is always close to or related to the founders and trained to take top positions or even to take over from the founder. This calls for a strong mentoring program in the organization, as previously discussed. Maggie shared that leadership mentoring is critical for leadership transition: candidates for senior positions are recruited from within rather than externally. Several other founders explained that they strive to have a well-designed mentoring program that offers a powerful and strategic tool for organizations to develop and retain talent within their own workforce.

8.3.1 Upholding Leadership Trust and Credibility

In the uncertain environment in which SENOs operate, leaders need to build or even rebuild trust and credibility with their constituents. Trust and credibility are important aspects of leadership in dual-mission organizations. The main component of credibility is honesty, and trust is closely linked to credibility. Trust in leadership is the belief followers have in the leader's integrity, character, and ability to deliver. Titus of Tonga noted that "as a leader, I am working with people who have not worked anywhere. I pick them from the village to work. This means that I need to build a trusting environment. I need to be honest in the way I deal with them." Therefore, character and integrity of the leadership, in addition to competency of the workforce, are an important influence on trust. Titus shared that he is open with the workforce and the donor community; he has nothing to hide with respect to their operations as a SENO.

The respondents repeatedly shared that leaders build trust through their character and competencies. While understanding the importance of character, Kelvin added, "You can have all the resources but if integrity is lacking, you cannot achieve your vision and mission. Leadership motivates staff. If all these things are put together, you can have a successful organization." In the same regard, Bill of CSE posited that trust results in a culture of high corroboration and a supportive work environment. The participants agreed that the perception of greater fairness contributes to trust in leadership. In this, the leaders support the staff and role modeling they provide to the workforce building higher trust levels to the workforce. Most participants share that they work hard to build an open policy organization where people are able to question the leadership when they feel it is not doing well. Mike of CAISD remarked that the leader's legitimacy equates to the confidence and trust subordinates feel in the leader. This trust is connected to leaders' behavior and ability to perform tasks.

The importance of trust is that trustworthy and credible leaders are competent and inspiring to the workforce and the external stakeholders. Stressing the significance of leaders' trustworthiness and credibility, Kelvin (CAISD) pointed out:

> We need to be trusted by our constituents. We have been in a situation where we lost trust with the donor community, both the organization and the enterprise were collapsing. So, we see the importance of being trustworthy and to be trusted. Even the staff are more committed when they trust the leadership. We have individuals who have stayed with us over 10 years because we are honest in the way we conduct our business.

Just like Kelvin, others also believed that employees' involvement in several organizations influences confidence and trust in leadership. Trust is further linked with positive job outcomes in the SENO. The SENOs' leaders understand that trust empowers the workforce to go beyond their capabilities and that an empowered workforce contributes more to the success of the entity. Huntsman and Greer (2019) agreed that trust in leadership improves the attitude and behavior of members and contributes to organizational effectiveness. Leadership trust helps in forming social exchange relations with members based on emotional support. Trust influences job performance and organizational citizenship behavior, which promotes the commitment of the individuals. The participants shared how credibility and honesty have helped them in staff retention and the commitment of their staff to doing the work.

Success or failure of any SENO falls on the leadership that is in place, so if workers cannot trust the leadership and if there is mistrust within the leadership team, it's quite difficult to see growth. Ben explained that leadership should drive the whole organization toward achieving the vision and the mission and making sure all resources are used as intended with integrity. Further, the study showed that trust in leadership increases the psychological well-being of the employees. The participants shared that the psychosocial well-being of the workforce reduces the desire of the individuals to leave the entity and promotes commitment. Trust in leadership is a predictor of organization commitment. The participants proudly shared that they have high staff retention rate because they are able to create what they call "a trusting family" in the organization.

8.4 Creating a Diverse Leadership Team

Social enterprising nonprofit organizations are increasingly finding the need to manage diversity within the changing demographic workforce. The research participants in this study shared that leadership diversity is a very important element in the success of the SENO. In modern terms, diversity management can be achieved when differences in organizations are acknowledged, accepted, and given a place in the integral structure and turned into a lifestyle. At the same time, proper management of diversity provides an environment where everyone can contribute to the organization and work toward the goals of the organization and where everyone has a potential to increase the firm's market share. Diversity management covers recognizing, accepting, respecting, utilizing, and being open to every kind of difference among the employees.

Findings show that diversity is the ability to embrace differences in the workforce. These differences can be in the form of gender, age, religion, ethnicity, and values, among others. In addition, diversity can be at either a surface or a deep level. Surface-level diversity includes the characteristics that are not difficult to observe. These characteristics include gender, physical capabilities, age, and disabilities. Meanwhile, deep-level diversity consists of aspects we cannot see at first glance. The deeper level diversity characteristics include religion, values, beliefs, and attitudes. The research participants indicated that leadership diversity is key in the successful operation of the organization. They highlighted that with the shifting demography, it becomes so imperative for the leaders to promote and support employee diversity. The study indicated that accepting proper management of diversity is a matter of life and death for the organizations. Proper management of work diversity helps organizations to expand core competencies. Dave, a founder of several SENOs, shared this observation:

> There is beauty in our differences, and we have come to a point where we have realized that we do need each other. We have been able to tolerate each other, agreeing with the ideas of one another, criticizing each other constructively then building each other in the process as we move forward.

The SENOs indicated that they deliberately plan a diverse work environment within the leadership. This is mostly done during the recruitment and selection process. They deliberately include minority and past discriminated groups when they are filling leadership positions in the organization. The findings revealed that some organizations deliberately employ women and youth in most of the top positions of the organization in order to balance the workforce. The organizations indicated that their effort is to deliberately create diverse leadership of the SENOs and thereby promote the performance of the SENO. Peter, whose organization focuses on equal employment opportunity, explained:

> As a school we hire both recent graduates and those who have retired from the government. We acknowledge the skills that the old employees will bring to the school. They are the ones who mentor these recent graduates, but it does not mean that these graduates bring nothing on the table. They have the modern knowledge of teaching and management that even help the older generation. In this we are creating a continuous learning process which helps in the performance of the employees.

In addition, the founders indicate that ethical behavior is key in creating diversity within the leadership of the organization. Several founders suggested that ethical values create an environment of equality in the organization. Equality, as Morand & Merriman (2012) articulated, fosters and maintains good interpersonal relationships. Furthermore, it helps promote integration in the workplace. This has an impact on planning and implementation of management practices, since it increases the commitment of the workforce to an organization. John of CYON shared:

> We promote an inclusive environment at every level of management. As a company, we value all types of diversity, and we treat people with equality. We know that if we treat people with respect and we do not discriminate in our hiring, then everyone else in the organization will do the same.

Equality is difficult to attain in most organizations because they are more rooted in equity or the sense that the outcomes individuals receive should be awarded in proportion to their inputs. The findings of this study indicate that equality comes from mature moral reasoning that is aimed at enhancing relationships in the organization and at the same time rewarding employees equally for their contributions. These findings suggest that values, when properly communicated and supported, can shape and guide employees in their ethical decision-making and interactions in an enterprise.

The interviews uncovered the idea that leadership helps in creating a cohesive and team-based organization. This is in line with Homan et al. (2020), whose research found that team leadership is vital in promoting, supporting, and developing team functions. The SENO founders in this study appreciated the importance of building a strong team with different skill sets in order to effectively implement their goals. The organizations indicated that team diversity promotes trust and compliance. Workplace diversity breeds creativity and innovation and presents group thinking. Above all, diversity reduces employee turnover and the associated cost of filling positions when people leave the organization. Yang & Konrad (2011) further shared that diversity in today's multigenerational, multiethnic, multiskilled workforce unites employees with different qualifications, backgrounds, and experience.

8.4.1 Commitment to the Organization's Vision

The SENO vision is central in the leadership of SENOs. Study participants believe that leadership's commitment to the vision is important in thriving SENOs. For the SENO, vision commitment is essential in being successful. The research participants believed that thriving in turbulent times rests on the extent to which leaders are committed to the organization's vision. Luke shared that running a successful organization calls for the leaders who believe in the vision and are willing to run with that vision, no matter the challenges. Most activities in the SENOs become static when there is a lack of commitment to vision by the leadership. He shared that "for one to run a successful organization, you firstly have to be focused, guided by the vision. The mission and vision underline the organization's activities in the achievement of the objectives."

This illustrates how leaders committed to a vision make it their passion; they have a heart to serve first and are committed to see change happening in the lives of those being served. This helps in turn to motivate employees to believe in the organizational vision. The founders shared that leaders in dual-mission organizations need to believe in the vision of the organization because it is this belief that makes the employees feel connected to the SENO.

Commitment of the leaders to the vision facilitates the commitment of the workforce to the same. The leader's desire to make the organization successful even in tough times plays a major role in the success of the organization. The heart of leadership is the belief that each leader has in the vision of the organization. William of RMM explained that the employees will mainly fit into the organization when there is vision commitment by the leaders. He said that leaders' commitment to vision creates a model of organizational citizenship behavior for the entire workforce. He contended:

> In the first place it is important for the organization to have clear goals of what you would want to achieve. As an organization, we are driven by those goals, and we are committed to see them accomplished. Our commitment brings trust to the followers because they know we are committed to achieving the goals.

The citizenship behavior motivates the workforce to do more toward the company's goals. Debora, the project manager at Hope Inc., concurred, sharing that she was driven to join the organization because she believed in the vision of the entity. But this belief, she said, came when she saw the commitment of the founders to the work. This kind of citizenship behavior from the leaders and the workforce drives SENOs' performance.

The leaders' "internal drive" to run a dual-mission organization has been an important element in the workforce commitment to the organization. This "internal drive" is the internally stimulated determination that the leaders have to make the vision successful. The research participants constantly mentioned that the internal driving force and the zeal to see the organization succeed are associated with how attached leaders are to the institution's vision. This means that leaders who are deeply rooted in their vision increase the motivation of the entire workforce in their work. Most leaders indicate that commitment comes when one is willing to serve beyond monetary gain. The commitment to serve communities is central to the SENOs' success in achieving their goals. Intrinsic satisfaction of the founders and top leaders has been key in holding the organization together. Dave, the founder of MSAHI, remarked:

> Building leadership is focusing on the vision, focusing on the mission, and making people to understand that satisfaction is not always in money. What we are trying to work on now, is to try and promote servant leadership, where you are looking at the satisfaction of anything that you are doing based on the broader good that you are going to get.

This means that leaders need not overlook extrinsic satisfaction though they can put much effort on intrinsic satisfaction. Outward satisfaction is central to the commitment to vision by the leaders. Therefore, rewarding accomplishments has been one of the strategies in enforcing leaders' commitment to the organization. The organizations see employees as being the strategic center for competitive advantage. Recognizing employees' efforts, success, and service is central to promoting commitment of the individuals in the organization. The participants believe that rewarding accomplishment improves workforce morale and at the same time helps in staff retention at the enterprise. The ability to keep happy staff and keep them over long periods of time helps in the flourishing of social enterprising nonprofit organizations.

8.5 Chapter Conclusion

Leadership is an important element in success and subsequent flourishing. The organizations strive to develop strong leaders that have strong entrepreneurial mindsets. Leaders do this by allowing employees to experiment with their ideas in the implementation of several activities. They promote teamwork, and they reward all forms of success. In addition, the organizations strategically engage in training and developing people that take on leading roles at all levels of an organization. The next chapter deals with entrepreneurial creativity and addresses matters of innovation, leadership in the market, and creativity in dealing with the external environment.

Chapter 9
Organizational Culture

Organizational culture plays an essential role in the success of any organization. The subsequent discussion follows the organization's culture as an element that propels the SENO toward flourishing. The themes cover several issues that create an organizational culture that facilitates flourishing: observing ethical operation standards, creating organizational shared values, establishing the flow of power, creating positive organizational climate, designing a just organization, and promoting a culture of innovation. The subsequent analysis seeks to address these issues as shared by the participants of this study.

9.1 Observing the Ethical Operation Standards

The founders frequently shared that they strive to build a culture around ethical standards. They believe that moral conduct of the institution is a critical component in running dual-mission organizations. In this regard, the organization's moral conduct means the implementation of proper policies and practices that inspire conduct that the organization should follow. Interviews revealed that ethical conduct both in the internal and external structures of the organization is integral to the operation and subsequent success of the organization. The findings suggest that the ethical standing of the organization helps to build trust with their community. Among the elements of ethical conducts are issues of honesty, transparency, integrity, and accountability. Several managers believed that these help in creating an organizational image that will either draw or drive people away. Mike of CAISD stressed:

> To run a successful organization, you have to be focused, guided by the vision, the mission, and underline your activities with the vision as well as the mission plus the proper leadership. This will help the organization to be transparent and accountable to the stakeholders. Transparency and accountability are important in maintaining the customers' loyalty.

Z. Chijere, *Nonprofit Social Enterprises*, CSR, Sustainability, Ethics & Governance, https://doi.org/10.1007/978-3-031-60234-4_9

This clearly indicates that developing a culture of honesty and trust is nonnegotiable. Concurring with this, Bruce highlighted the importance of being honest with his workforce: "One thing which we have found very crucial is that you have to be up front and very frank with all your employees." This indicates that the behavior and attitudes of individuals in the organization strongly depend on how honest the organization is in their dealings with both internal and external stakeholders. Several managers explained that they had invested a lot in creating a positive environmental context by being honest with the workforce.

These interviews with the founders suggest that integrity is an essential ethical element to which social enterprising organizations need to adhere. Organizations that are living well promote high levels of integrity in their conduct. It has been established that integrity in an organization increases trust among the members and their leadership. As discussed earlier, trust in leadership is a moderating factor for organizational citizenship and promotes creativity in the workforce. It is integrity that further increases the trustworthiness of the entity from the external stakeholders. Luka of CDECO discussed integrity in terms of encounters with donors:

> Integrity and accountability are key for sustainable institutions. People have to see (that) you are trustworthy…because that's the accusations that NGOs get. We are accused of not being accountable and that we lack integrity in our dealings…therefore, in promoting organizational integrity and upholding the ethical standards, it helps us to be trusted by our clients and even our staff.

Several managers concurred that ethical living helps organizations to build a culture that propels them to success by creating an institution concerned with establishing good relations with its workforce and those within its impact. In this, the managers shared that ethical living brings out strong engagement of people in the organization's activities. Success of the organization to some extent depends on the level of commitment from staff. As William of RMM explained:

> You can have all the required resources for the organization. However, if you do not have the commitment of the staff, it will be hard to succeed. You need the commitment from the people. You need the staff to be highly involved in the implementation of the organizational goals.

This argument further shows that ethical conduct helps the employees believe in the leadership of the organization, which in turn promotes their level of commitment. Interviews with the founders and directors showed that creating ethically acceptable behaviors in the organization helps people to commit and truly engage themselves with the work. The leaders interviewed believe that ethical living creates a trusting environment inside the organization, which is vital in holding it together. Findings suggest that employees who have a strong trust in their leadership and managers are obligated to give more to the organization. This is also well supported in several previous studies. Peter, et al (2019), for example, argued that ethical conduct helps in improving the firm's reputation for both internal and external constituents. The participants in this study contended that any SENO's reputation impacts both the internal and external competitiveness of the organization. First, it influences the individual engagement in the activities of the organization because of trust in the organization. The good standing that the organization has in the community also influences growth, since individuals will be more committed to the affairs of the organization. In addition, the reputation of the organization influences its networks and all stakeholders. The organization needs suppliers, donors, customers, and investors. The social standing of the institution toward these stakeholders can distinguish the organization from its competitors. The organization that ethically stands above others easily wins support from the desired networks.

9.1.1 Creating Organizational Shared Values

The analyzed data reveal that organizational values are one of the building blocks of organizational culture for SENOs. Workplace values are the guiding principles that are integral to how the organization works. Values are further regarded as basic convictions about what is right, good, or desirable. In this, values help the organization to understand what good conduct is expected by their community. Findings from the interviews suggest that values are the standards of behavior that help the organization define what is important in their operation. This means that organizational values represent the foundation on which the organization is built and are the important uniting elements of the organization. It is the values that determine organizational conduct on judging what is important to the organization. Hence, it is values that create the architecture of the organization that defines behavior within and outside the organization. Dave of MSAHI rightly said:

> You cannot break them (values), they are natural principles; they are natural laws. You can't break them, but you can break yourself against them, so by building everything on a value-based system, success doesn't become a problem because everything is value based, everything that you are doing is based on the values.

Just as this manager points out, the organizational culture that is built on clear values has the potential to succeed in its activities. This is because values help the organization to build the framework on the behaviors of the organization. Findings from the founders indicate that they transfer these values to the entire organization by the way leaders live their lives and through verbal communication. Concurring with this, Kelvin of CAISD stressed:

> We have values that we'll have to guard jealously.... we need to share the values of organization with all members of the organization. We value ethical conduct with all our staff because it is through the values that we have that we are able to have a united team. Everyone else knows and they abide by it.

This founder believes that values are an important building block in creating strong working relationships among staff members. At the end of the day, dual-mission organizations need a workforce that is closely knit together, one in which people feel that each of them is part of a bigger family. When it comes to building a strong unit in organizations, Bruce of Tonga remarked:

> I do believe we are able to attract new people in the organization because we are a value-based organization. At the same time, we have stayed together as a team because we do respect our values. So, this culture has helped us in the staff retention and attracting more people into the organization.

The study's findings further suggest that values link the organization as a unit since values help to build trust within the organization. Beyond that, values enable the SENO to create an identity that helps them to market themselves in the industry. Several managers shared that the goal is to build the organization on value systems. There is a need to develop strategy and engage all the stakeholders in creating these values; otherwise, it can be very tricky, especially if the organization does not have clear standards of behavior. The managers shared their belief that if the organization is not built on principles and values, it can be a source of mismanagement at some level, so it is important that it be built on a value system at various levels.

Trust is the positive expectation regarding others' conduct. Trust is an essential element in the management of dual-mission organizations, since it fosters bonding between individuals and creates a sense of responsibility toward others. The research participants indicated that a trusting environment has been an important element in creating a strong organizational culture. Both leaders and managers in successful SENOs spend much time making sure that they create a trusting environment inside and outside the organization. Luke of CDECO narrated how they had once gone through the distress of mistrust by the public:

> The first thing we want is to build trust. We have been in that situation where people have lost trust in us to the point of claiming their money back. That's why we strive to always earn the trust of the people by being a trusted institution.

Both interview data and organizational observations showed that trust directly affects employees' morale, productivity, and innovation and lack of trust leads to counterproductive employee behaviors in the organization. Some of these counterproductive behaviors include corruption and lack of commitment to the organization, both of which have negative impacts on the flourishing of the organizations. Individual perceptions of an organization's behavior trigger either positive or negative attitudes toward the institution's flourishing.

Ozyilmaz et al. (2019) indicated that low trust influences employee intentions to leave the organization, which negatively affects performance. Findings from the interviews further suggest that organizational trust helps the organizations in staff retention and citizenship behavior from the employees. The leadership and organizations that have high trust from their stakeholders are able to keep staff longer in the organization, which helps in transferring organizational knowledge to the new recruits, something essential to success. Several founders explained that it is difficult to retain staff, especially in the nonprofit sector characterized by low pay. However, building a culture of trust helps in retaining staff and at the same time attracting more talent to the organization. Furthermore, trust reduces the intention of the individuals to leave the organization. Above all, trust has a positive effect on job satisfaction, task performance, and citizenship behavior, essential elements of organizational success.

Trust is a positive influencer in the workplace in terms of psychological safety. The participants discussed their belief that the individual perception of security in their job influences their commitment to give their best to the institution. Trust improves employees' attitude toward work, and that helps in improving workforce behavior, attitude, and performance. In contrast, lack of trust induces the perception of risk and uncertainty. It in turn triggers the behavior of self-interest and work deviance (Page et al., 2019; Thau et al., 2007). Furthermore, trust is a contributing factor to an individual's self-efficacy in the SENO. According to Bandura, one's self-efficacy plays a major role in how one approaches tasks, goals, and challenges. Bandura (1998) perceived self-efficacy as people's beliefs in their capabilities to produce designated levels of performance that influence their lives. It affects how people feel, think, motivate themselves, and behave. The SENOs indicate that the behavior of employees in their self-belief and confidence to produce a certain level of performance is dictated by the trusting environment created by the founders or top leaders in the organization.

9.2 The Flow of Power

Power dynamics and the flow of information are an important element of culture that facilitates success for the organization. Several participants underscored the fact that power is one of the tools that is essential to management of a profit-making nonprofit organization; an organization will not exist without power relations. Power can be defined as the ability to marshal human, informational, or material resources to get something done. Diffusion of power in the organization influences relationships within the organization and determines the work attitudes of the individuals. Henry of CSE, focusing on how managers use power in SENOs, stressed: "Power goes with integrity. We have been in situations where managers wrongly used power by intimidating others. We lost so many good employees until we realized that someone was not using power wisely." He further noted, "We are open on how we deal with the staff. We give them enough information on whatever is happening in the organization. They have enough information on all the decisions that concerns them."

Organizational power is moderated by the type of structure that the SENOs adopt. Highlighting the flow of power and information, Bill shared: "We try to create a flatter organization structure. The staff should feel they are part and parcel of the company, they should not feel that they are working for the company but own it." The participants agreed on the importance of both horizontal and vertical power relations in the organization. Distribution of power influences how committed the individuals are to the activities of the enterprise. The more the employees feel that they have power, the more they are committed to the organization. Power diffusion moderates the organizational citizenship behavior of the subordinates. Mike of CAISD also concurred with others on the flow of power and information, saying:

> We deliberately delegate responsibilities to the managers in various companies we own. This helps to share responsibility in decision making and when things go wrong it is not one person to blame but everybody. As leaders we are committed to foster success by empowering each individual working with us. Nothing for us is more empowering than seeing people with power and energy in the entire system.

Power affects how decisions are made in the organization. Diffusing power through delegation helps the SENOs become effective in decision-making because it is a shared activity. The participants believe that when power is diffused, it empowers the managers to make decisions at all levels of the organization rather than depending on the founders alone. Bill of CSE rightly observed:

> You have heard the story of NASA, where a visitor, upon finding an office cleaner, asked him, "Oh, what do you do here?" The cleaner answered, "I am sending a rocket to the moon." The cleaner believed that he was as good as an engineer. He believed that he was not just there to make tea and clean the offices, rather he considered himself as part of a system, an important aspect in helping his organization operate efficiently. That's the culture we have.

Although several founders shared the importance of diffusing power, findings revealed that some dual-mission organizations in this study concentrate power in one or a few individuals. These organizations find it difficult to innovate in the enterprise because power is concentrated in a few individuals. Henry, one of the managers at MSAHI, complained that since more power is concentrated in the founder than the management team, they are discouraged from innovating and taking initiative in the organization. At the same time, this demotivates the individuals and undermines commitment to the organization. Unequal distribution of power creates a climate of fear of failure, which affects performance.

The flow of information is also an important aspect of the flourishing of a SENO. Kelvin CAISD explained how the information flows in their organization, saying:

> We ensure the smooth flow of information in the organization. We do regular meetings as an enterprise. In fact, we have weekly meetings with the teachers where they are able to share their feelings on the operations of the school.

He continued, saying that even a cleaner comes to his office not to gossip but to share their feelings on how things are working. This gives the management team a good feedback system to help create more products and services.

9.3 Creating Positive Organizational Climate

Organizational climate is a shared perception of what the organization is like in terms of practices, policies, procedures, routines, and rewards. This shared perception among employees on the policies, procedures, and practices in the organization creates either a favorable environment for the workforce or not. The interviews suggest that a positive perception of the work environment in the organization is essential to the subsequent success of the entity, a supposition well supported in the literature. Several managers asserted that a good working climate induces positive behavior from the employees in an organization. The interviews with the founders and directors clearly showed that the organizational climate creates an environment that either promotes citizenship behavior or not. All research participants indicated that their ability to keep employees and attract more employees is strongly linked to how the individuals like their working environment. A successful organization creates policies and procedures that will keep a happy workforce. For instance, one organization, among many other things, has a policy that allows teachers to bring their children or close relatives to learn for free at their institution. This increases the commitment of the workforce, since they know firsthand that the organization has programs that benefit their welfare.

Organizational climate affects the stress of the employees in the organization. Maggie shared that it often becomes essential for the dual-mission organization to create an internal organizational climate that promotes emotional and mental well-being in the workforce. To do this, the organization must create strategies that reduce the stress levels that come with the related work in the organization because their employees' mental condition is valuable in the performance of the entity. Findings showed that effective leaders create an organization that supports the mental health of the individual worker. The ability to create these systems is an important element in creating a suitable work environment. The participants promote programs and policies that will help the mental health of the individual. They highlighted the fact that they create transparent organizations. Staff are free to ask questions and even to share their thoughts on behaviors. Luke said: "We are an open organization where people are able to tell us where we are not doing well. We are even able to accept criticism, although sometimes we stand our ground and do things our way after evaluation of the idea that was brought forth." Such an environment where people are able to express their feeling has been essential in reducing work-related stress. The open organizational policy has helped individual employees to assist each other and at the same time has allowed organizations to look into the welfare of its employees.

Leadership is important in creating a good working environment and inspiring the workforce. Leadership approach creates an organization climate that motivates people to have a desire to be associated with the organization. Several managers shared their belief that democratic approaches to leadership give the individual employee an opportunity to question and even make suggestions about working conditions. Leaders open to accommodating views and inviting managers to share their thoughts on policies and procedure are more successful in creating an acceptable organizational climate. Henry of MSAHI shared that leadership has been the main component in creating a good organizational climate:

> You can have all the resources but if you do not have integrity, you cannot achieve your vision and the mission of your organization will never be achieved. Leadership must motivate staff, and if all those things are put together, you can find that you can have a successful organization.

He added:

> I have seen such a culture: where we live as a community, people relate well and trust each other. They are able to share experiences, and, in that way, we are able to help one another, even socially. Even academically, people are able also to share their challenges through that good relation culture. We are able to see where others can come in to cover maybe where they feel they are not competent so that we ensure smooth running or smooth delivery of maybe lessons in the classrooms.

In addition, collaboration among different players in the organization has been a pertinent component of creating a good organizational climate. The organizations believe that working together as a team has propelled them into success. Cooperation among staff members is one element of a good working organizational climate for the employees. The leaders remarked that collaboration among employees helps bring out the best in workers. Collaboration has helped many individuals to use their talents in the organization. The unity and understanding among employees help balance the focus of individuals in organizational activities. Steven, the SE manager at CYE, said:

> It's just as the saying goes that united, we stand divided we fall. We work as a team, there is that strength that diversity brings. You know for instance all these companies that are coming are a result of passions from different directors within the organization.

The clearly shared goals and organizational policies help in creating collaboration among individuals in the organization. The participatory nature of an organization calls for clarification of roles. This is further elaborated by Shen and Zhang (2019), who contend that the extent of a leader's ability to create an ethical organization determines the willingness of the employees to collaborate.

9.4 Designing a Just Organization

Issues of justice are pertinent when it comes to creating a sustainable and acceptable organizational culture in the SENO. Justice is perceived fairness in the processes and procedures of the organization (Neveu & Kakavand, 2019). The findings from this study suggest that just behavior and treatment help to create a system that is well respected and trusted by stakeholders. Individuals' perception of how justly they are treated at work influences their innovation and attitude toward productivity. Perceived just or unjust treatment triggers a corresponding attitude toward work from the employees. That is why the dual-mission organization in this research sees the importance of creating a just organization. Proving the significance of justice in the organizations, Luke of CDECO says:

> I believe that every person desires an environment where people are treated with fairness. In order for us to create that environment we encourage people's commitment to the organization. The just environment helps the workforce to be dedicated and productive in our work here.

Staff members' perception of fairness of the organization will influence their inclination toward the violation of the organization norms and acts of deviance behavior toward their work. Justice in combined-mission organizations is seen in the reward system in place. Bruce of MSAHI concurs with this assertion:

> Being able to pay the staff fairly and reward them on time helps us to keep most of our staff. So, we make sure that no matter what, we give our people fair wages and a rewarding working environment. We are committed to the growth of the individuals in all our enterprises. We treat individuals with respect and dignity regardless of the position they hold in this organization.

This means that a fair reward system promotes task performance and citizenship behavior in the organization. Several individuals suggested that how the reward system is viewed by employees reveals a great deal about how employees are valued. The argument resonates with the views in the literature. Neveu and Kakavand (2019) contend that workplace deviance is closely linked with organizational justice. Deviant behaviors are manifested in the workforce through corrupt practices and noncommitment to adhering to the organizational practices and procedures. The SENOs investigated realize that creating a fair environment is essential in creating a dedicated workforce. Titus, a SENO founder, said that their focus is on creating good ethical standards for all employees: "We make sure that we adhere to our philosophy. When our employees fail to adhere to the ethical standards it affects their dedication which result into a poor working environment and affects their productivity." The importance of policies to safeguard the guidelines of the organizations cannot be understated. Such policies help managers to form guidelines on how best they treat each individual in the company. Kelvin explained: "We are guided by policies which are our guiding documents of behavior here. I believe this facilitates fairness in how we resolve issues and on how we distribute resources in the organization."

9.4.1 Promoting a Culture of Innovation and Creativity

Organizations that flourish have built a strong culture of innovation in all departments. In successful organizations, innovation is promoted and supported by top management, as highlighted previously in the literature section of this study. The participants extensively proved the direct relationship between increased perception of entrepreneurial culture and employee level of output. Several founders regarded innovation as the most important aspect that drives effectiveness of dual-mission organizations. Findings revealed that the culture that promotes individual behavior to try out their ideas inside the organization motivates a friendly internal environment that fosters innovation. In the same vein, Ireland et al. (2006) found that an innovative friendly culture fosters innovative behavior from the workforce. Dave (MSAHI) indicated that they work hard to create an atmosphere in which innovative ideas are accommodated in the organization: "We motivate our staff to think of ideas on how we can do things better through their respective positions. As an organization, we reward the individuals who have innovative ideas." Rewarding innovative and creative behaviors is instrumental in promoting innovation among staff. In agreement with the several founders, Henry from MSAHI expressed his view that rewards reinforce innovative behavior and encourage the workforce to meet challenges in the entity. Organizational cultures that allow individuals to experiment with their ideas lead to more innovators and creative implementation of activities.

The happy living organizations in this study deliberately create a culture where individuals are free to think and experiment. Bruce of MSAHI explained that their entity "provides a platform through which staff at all levels are able to provide feedback and that is done through promoting and encouraging meetings in all the departments." Work autonomy creates a culture that motivates employees to innovate. Successful organizations tolerate failure as they allow freedom in how the employees carry out their work. Effective organizations create a learning culture in which they are able not only to delegate responsibilities but also support a learning culture through their structures. Linda of Hope Inc. agreed with these sentiments, saying, "We give people the freedom to propose or give ideas regarding the work they are doing. We welcome any ideas and support them if need be. This helps our staff to operate in a free environment where they are free to propose any ideas they have."

It is interesting to note how one SENO involves the artisans in the whole process of creating new products and strategies. The ability for the artisans to learn from each other and provide creativity is one intriguing part of their process, showing how open and friendly the internal system is in providing opportunities for staff to innovate. The manager of one SENO in the production sector explained how they are geared to foster creativity: "fostering creativity is one of our objectives as we continue to expand. For example, we are now making toys using pasta packets." Sharing their organization's approach to creating innovation culture, Linda of Hope Inc. went further:

> We have given a bit of independence to the individual teams, whilst of course they may need to refer to us in some cases; there is a sense of flexibility. We give them that mandate to propose and suggest ideas. Then we are able to endorse their ideas, although others will do without endorsing as long as they are making positive contributions to the company.

This suggests that there is a big connection between staff independence and innovation in SENOs. The more independent the staff, the more they are able to create new ideas that promote the performance of the organization. When managers are completely empowered, they are ambitious to meet targets and grow as if they are growing their personal business. The founders challenge SENO leaders to create an internal environment that fosters autonomy to influence ongoing innovative culture. The SENOs strive to create an internal climate that motivates individuals to be more innovative. Bolman and Deal (2017) called culture the glue that holds the organization together. They said culture comprises the underlying beliefs, assumptions, values, and ways of interrelating that contribute to the unique psychological and social atmosphere of the organization. In most cases, culture is regarded as the personality of the organization because it is a system of shared beliefs and values that defines the behavior of the organization. An organization's culture defines the identity of the organization and helps to create organizational behavior.

9.5 Chapter Conclusion

Organizational culture is among the key factors in the flourishing of SENOs. This study shows that organizations that are flourishing have good organizational climate that promotes innovation and creativity among employees. Beyond this, the flourishing entities focus on building ethical organizations. They deliberately put measures into place that help the personnel to adhere to the ethical conduct in the organization. They do this by having written out policies and codes of conduct that are shared among all employees.

Chapter 10
Entrepreneurial Creativity

Entrepreneurial creativity is a significant factor in the flourishing of SENOs. It involves leaders and the whole workforce being innovative, understanding the external environment so as to deal with that environment in a way that benefits the SENO, and having significant influence on the market for both the charity and social enterprising part of a SENO. These three factors lead to an organization that is functioning well. The following analysis addresses these three important factors.

10.1 The Role of Innovation in SENO Flourishing

Interview findings showed that dual-mission organizations are continually embracing innovation as a central principle for survival and flourishing. Innovation is one of the central aspects of the flourishing SENO. We can liken innovation to the biological process of mutation, which keeps species abreast in the survival race. This means that innovation helps the organization to remain relevant in an ever-changing operating environment. In this study, innovation was observed both in the charity and the business section of the SENO. In the modern-day operation of organizations, innovation needs to be observed even in charitable organizations. Study participants believed that any dual-mission organization needs to bring constant innovation into their operations for the success of the organization. Innovation is seen either in creating new ideas or improving existing ideas to enhance performance, quality, or durability of the products/services. The following discussion focuses on different dimensions of innovation that the study uncovered in flourishing SENOs in Malawi. These dimensions include demonstrating strategic thinking, investing in research and development, achieving evolutionary and/or disruptive innovation, and involving community in the innovation. Innovation in this section encompasses how both the charity and the economic ventures innovate in their operation.

Z. Chijere, *Nonprofit Social Enterprises*, CSR, Sustainability, Ethics
& Governance, https://doi.org/10.1007/978-3-031-60234-4_10

10.1.1 Demonstrating Strategic Thinking

The feeling among several managers and founders was that the goal of innovation is to create strategic advantage for the organization over their competitors. The organization needs individuals who are strategic thinkers to innovate new strategies and approaches in doing work. Understanding a fast-changing environment requires identifying strategies, analyzing customer value requirements, and conducting strategic segmentation. The ability to analyze a fast-changing environment is key to the success of dual-mission organizations in their quest for innovation. Strategic thinking helps leaders to identify gaps in their operations and to picture how they can uniquely fill those gaps effectively and efficiently. Mike of CAISD proudly said, "We believe that we are a champion service provider. We call ourselves champions because we have always introduced initiatives. We are champions in innovations because we allow individual to think in the operations of the organization." He shared that CAISD is the first organization to focus on irrigation and water technology. The Executive Director highlighted that the ability to think sets them apart from the rest in their industry. He shared that creating value calls for the leaders to think beyond the status quo, as did Steven, a top manager at CSE who said that they excel despite bad industry conditions because they focus on creating opportunities in their fields rather than being victims of those conditions. It is the same response given by several other SENOs who focus on dictating the business approach in their industry, which requires individuals who are able thinkers in their operations.

Strategic thinking helps the SENO to come up with innovative for-profit ventures that bring money to the charity work. Rather than merely copying from other organizations, business ideas in the SENO come after a long thoughtful process in which leaders have to assess the organization's capacity as well as community needs. The findings suggest that most businesses and charity works are not copied but created by individuals within an organization who are capable of thinking on ways to generate revenue. Luke of CAISD shared that the business part came in after they had operated as a charity for about 3 years. They had been dependent on donors for their operation.

They later realized that depending on donors alone was limiting them to some extent because they couldn't meet the vision of the organization with donor money constraints. He said: "We had to implement other organizations using our own resources, and that is when we proposed on doing our own business for sustainability purposes." Understanding the fast-changing market requires the SENO to identify new ways of doing things. This calls for the leaders' strategic thinking, the mental process that helps them to innovate approaches to their operation. The framework of strategic thinking motivates the SENO to form strategic initiatives that help them to remain relevant in the community. Interview data revealed that the strategic thinking process in a successful organization is both rational and intuitional. In rationality, strategic thinking follows a process in the creation of approaches, while in intuition the thinking favors instant approaches.

Study participants remarked that strategic thinking should be embraced across the organization, which requires good coordination in the internal system of the SENO. Dave, the founder of MSAHI, explained:

> As for us, constant inter-departmental communication helps our enterprise in promoting the thinking process of new ideas and at the same time breaking possible barriers to innovations. The communication helps in facilitating good interaction between the department and we are able to create interventions for the benefit of the entire company.

Strategic thinking should be embraced at all levels of the organization. This study shows that leaders need to enforce strategic thinking by constantly engaging and challenging individuals in the organization to innovate. The leaders that support innovative behaviors influence the organization-wide innovative behaviors because individuals understand that experimenting is accepted in the organization.

On the other hand, the findings from the interviews show that there are no shortcuts or quick fixes in the flourishing of the SENO. That is why strategic thinking is vital. In principle, the participants shared that this calls for both deductive and inductive reasoning for the managers of the firms. Both deductive and inductive reasoning help the dual-mission organization resist the temptation for instant gratification in whatever they do. One manager shared how they took over 4 years of planning to venture into social enterprising. They spent a lot of time learning the procedures of running social businesses. Several founders further indicated that they took a year to pilot their strategy before its actual implementation. This indicates the need for leaders to take time in creating the business idea and its subsequent operationalization. The emphasis of organization innovation as the foundation of success pushes leaders and manager to create an institution that will deliberately embrace strategic thinking as a tool for success. To be innovative and strategic, the organizations need to do proper research in their industry.

10.2 Being Innovative: Investing in Research and Development

Several interviewees explained that research and development is an important element in the innovation process of dual-mission organizations. Research and development help the organization to conduct innovative problem- or opportunity-focused research within the organization but concerning the external environment. Innovation for SENOs comes from understanding what works in the industry and their stakeholders' value requirements. Small nonprofit organizations invest little in research and development, which in turn affects their innovation behavior. However, SENOs that see the value of research and development are rich in internal understanding of their activities and can thus engage with the external environment informatively, which in turn positively influences their innovative behaviors. The Art Box Ltd. Creative Director remarked:

> As an organization, we invest in research. We make sure that we include research in our budget line. We started investing into research and development when we realized that we were becoming irrelevant to our customers since there was no any kind of improvement in the products we were putting on the market.

In agreement, Phillip of CYON said:

> We constantly compare the knowledge with what is not working on the market which helps us to understand the gaps. We need to study and understand what our customers are looking for. This helps us to create products that uniquely meet the demands of our customers.

Findings suggest that researching and understanding the environment is paramount in all SENOs. All the SENOs that are flourishing invest heavily in research. The organizations deliberately create procedures to obtain information that will help them in their operations. CSE's founder shared that they had a Ph.D. candidate who helped them to do a study on their operations to see the gaps in their organization. This helped them to get information that they used in improving or creating new approaches in their organization. He shared that several interventions they are now conducting emerged from the results of that study. Commenting on the significance of research in coming up with a new and unique product, the Hope Inc. founder explained:

> We do research before we create any product. This helps in understanding the marketability of the product; we do not want to create a product that will not meet the needs of our customers. The research mostly helps to understand the customer's values and see the changes in the society.

This justifies the fact that the SENOs that are able to read market trends and devise means to be relevant in the market are those that flourish. Just like Bruce of Hope Inc., several founders shared that that innovation for their SENO is strongly dependent on external knowledge. They believe that firms cannot entirely rely on internal knowledge and experience for innovation. Innovation is strongly associated with the performance of the firm's R&D.

Furthermore, SENOs are able to use individuals outside the organization to provide expertise on what can work and how it can work. For CSE, the ability to consult has been one of the great contributors to the development and subsequent success of the organization. CYON shared that when they were looking for profit-making opportunities, "the radio became an option for the organization. This was done after a vast consultation and understanding on what could help them to generate that income. We involved individuals who had been in the broadcasting industry to help us the setting of the whole station." For them, gaining competitive intelligence has been key to the success of the SENO. CYON's founder indicated that consultation helps them adapt to external environment complexities in improving their market performance. The SENOs indicate that this R&D approach helps them to improve their market performance, since they are able to provide client-focused products/services. Participants shared that their success is dependent on the acquisition of external knowledge from their environment. The ability to gather and analyze the product/service performance helps in the strategic approach of the SENOs.

The findings from interviews with the founders showed that innovation requires money. The participants stressed the fact that investing in the innovation of the firm significantly affects its economic development. In the same regard, Luke of CAISD indicated that a firm's investment in innovation leads to the creation of innovative culture. Those dual-mission organizations that are flourishing are continually investing in innovation. The organizations are willing to take the risk of allowing their employees to experiment with ideas. For experimenting to happen, the SENOs invest money in promoting innovative ideas in the enterprise. Luke of CAISD explained:

> The availability of resources for us is the building block for innovation. We work on funding individuals who come up with creative ideas that we know if successful will bring us money. The digital document saving business was an idea from some of our students. We were willing to fund their idea and because of this, we are promoting the innovation culture around here. The enterprise bears the cost of institution innovations and if necessary, we invest in purchasing innovation.

To be innovative, then, organizations need to invest heavily in individuals with experimental ideas. This study indicated that innovation calls for a lot of serious investment with a well-built network both within and outside the organization. With respect to the radio station, Phillip indicated: "Radio calls for intensive resource mobilization and capital injections in order to run issues like transmitters so that you have widespread coverage." Y-Radio has deliberately invested in the operation of the enterprise to become a national radio station, as it is the only SENO in Malawi that operates a national radio station. The investment is helping the radio to be more successful than their counterparts. They have won the trust of their clients and the donor community. Investing in innovation attracts more institutional capital, which contributes to the scale of the economy of the SENO. Titus indicated that for them to make their dreams a reality, they had to invest in their ideas, as he clearly narrates:

> For this business, we have one major supporter, which is the family of my late son's family. They are the ones who have done a lot on the development of the lodge. They invested a lot in the project, and they have helped us to achieve this project, without them we wouldn't be talking about this 4 Star hotel in the bush. It was just an idea; with investment it became a reality. So, I do the same with my managers. I support them financially when they have an idea to make our lodge grow.

Several founders and top managers agreed that investing in innovation raises the success of the organization. It is regarded as a tool that helps the organization to be different from other organizations but also to be relevant in the community they are working.

10.3 Evolutionary and/or Disruptive Innovation

The findings from the interviews uncover two types of innovations that are happening in the flourishing organizations: evolutionary and disruptive innovation. The first type of innovation is called evolutionary innovation. This study established that for a business to succeed, SENOs should focus on continuous innovation. Kumar et al. (2020) assert that successful organizations focus on constant innovation in order to remain relevant in the industry. Evolutionary innovation focuses on continuously offering value products/services compared to competitors' offerings. This idea entails constantly satisfying stakeholders with improved products/services. Several organizations ensure that they are introducing innovative products/services now and again. Linda of Hope Inc. said that to survive and flourish in the industry, they keep on dreaming and implementing new ideas for the existing product and for creating new business ventures as well as expanding their charity work. She further explains the innovations of their entity as she says that, at their center, they want to start a cafeteria where people can have breakfast and lunch weekdays but also on Saturdays and Sundays. She explained:

> We make it as vibrant as it can be with music to direct traffic from Lilongwe to the refugee camp. We will also market the work that we are doing. We will be showing the refugee camp as having…a lot of zeal and positivity to life but also to generate income that we need for the organization and the people we are serving.

She continued, explaining that the organization itself is growing by introducing new products and improved approaches to work. Linda indicated that social enterprising nonprofit organizations in constant innovation are able to overcome their industry's tough conditions. For Hope Inc., they are able to create opportunities by incremental improvement through adding value to their products and services. This indicates that running a social enterprising organization calls for creativity and of course thoughtfulness regarding what is being done. Debora, a manager within the same organization, concurred, sharing that they do this every time in order to be different in what they are doing, especially in the craft industry, where they need to create new products every time they are bringing new stock to the market. Phillip of CYCON agreed:

> It is not cheap and not easy to sustain a media house like a radio station. Just like a TV station or newspapers, the biggest challenge is that if every time any station or any media house has an audience and you take that audience for granted, it is the first step to lose the audience. We need to keep on innovating to keep our audience.

Evolutionary innovation helps Y-Radio keep customers and even attract new ones in the business section of the SENO. This continuous innovation keeps the SENO on its toes, making sure that they remain relevant to the customers and to the industry. John of CYON reported, "Every day they come up with a new thing because they do not want people who have bought their product to get out of the shop empty handed, but at to have their product of some kind. This prompts us to constantly come up with new things." Henry contends that continuous quality improvement improves company performance and profitability. This means that continuous innovation will affect the profitability and performance of the entity in its environment. Therefore, SENO must see a systematic process of incremental and ongoing innovation to assure the long-term viability and competitiveness of the organization.

The second type of innovation is disruptive innovation. According to Schumpeter (1949), disruptive innovation refers to a technology whose application significantly affects the way the industry functions. In simple terms, it is the innovation that creates new markets for the products/services and displaces existing practices in the industry. Many of the SENOs are using approaches and theories of disruptive innovation, which have enabled some of the SENOs to dislodge some big companies in the industry. A few SENOs in this study are breaking away from traditional ways of thinking and embracing disruptive innovation as a way of developing new business growth. Findings show that although it can be risky to break away from tradition, doing so gives a better chance for SENOs to be more competitive in the market. Flourishing SENOs take the risk of going into an industry that is difficult to enter and uniquely create an intervention that dislodges traditional business approaches.

The secret for many SENOs in their disruptive approaches is to trust their abilities. Mike of CAISD, whose SENO has significantly changed the industry, said: "We do not doubt ourselves and we have the confidence…we are currently moving into agricultural financing bank sector. Our banking enterprise is different from the traditional bank." They saw an opportunity that was not tested in their industry, the agricultural financing bank. No bank at that time solely focused on financing local farmers. Beyond financing, they also offer free finance coaching and modern agricultural training to their clients. This has set them apart in the industry, and others find it difficult to imitate. Highlighting the significance of doing things differently, one participant shared their disruptive approach in digital document saving, a new and foreign approach in Malawi. Bill, one of the founders of CSE, remarked:

> Recently we have registered a financial services company where we are digitizing documents especially for the banks. For example, last year we have digitized documents for First Capital Bank. All their documents are digitalized in a way that they are put in a DMA system that is now in a server to enable anybody within First Capital Banks anywhere to access anything that they want.

This has helped CSE to become a leading social enterprising nonprofit organization in their industry. CSE has been a leading organization in digital data saving, which is changing the landscape of doing data saving in Malawi. Bill asserts that disruptive innovation has the potential to reinvent a product by introducing a new attribute that could become a key source of competitiveness for the firm. CSE has made the effort to reinvent what is happening in developed countries and apply it to local contexts. Instead of paper filing, most big banks and leading firms are moving into digital data saving. Just as the CSE Executive Director shared, their disruptive approach in the industry helps them to reinvent by offering products/services with a different package of attributes that easily displace established competitors.

In disruptive innovation, SENOs allow their employees to think outside the box in order to bring off-the-shelf components into their products. The Hope Inc. Creative Director indicated that they utilize any resource in order to produce something unique. She said:

> We design crafts and commission the manufacturing of crafts and these are largely {our} design crafts. We also have some that are more traditional woven items using sisal, some of

> the items are made using plywood and many items utilize household waste. We even re-use waste such as the Pasta Packet, Likuni Phala packet or OMO Washing Powder.

Hope Inc. also repurposes plastic water bottles, reutilizing the boxes of cereals and other things as part of sustainable tourism. A manager says this approach originated from their artisans. They know that the organization-wide approach to innovation has propelled them to create new and unique products. O'Reilly and Binns (2019) notes three disciplines for disruptive innovation: ideation, incubation, and scaling. For SENOs like Hope Inc., generating new business ideas, which is ideation, has been key to the growth and success of the organization. They are creative in thinking of producing something from whatever raw material is available to change how people create crafts in Malawi. Like many other SENOs, Hope Inc. focuses on displacing the established paradigm in the craft industry in Malawi. This is what Mike and his friends at CAISD explained: disruptive innovation intends to dislodge the status quo by making the old techniques redundant. Hope Inc., CAISD, CYON, CSE, and Tonga Foundation all embrace the idea of shaking up previously successful approaches by creating new ideas for them to survive and flourish in their industry.

The founders realized that being aggressive and different in the way they provide their services/products has been one of the unique features of their disruptive approach of doing business. The SENOs are able to reallocate their assets and capabilities to see the growth of their ideas. Titus of Tonga Foundation observed that the real change for them is to create unique products that will succeed in the market and help them run their charities:

> We ventured into eco-lodge industry with a 4-star hotel. The concept is new in the country and not many even commercial companies venture into this. But we realized that for us to be unique, we need to be thinking differently.

Highlighting the uniqueness of their innovation, he proudly explained, "Here at Tonga, you are in a bush, but you are in a 4 Star Hotel…you are surrounded by the bushes, all alone in the middle of nowhere, along the river." SENOs that are flourishing are unique in innovating business ideas to disrupt the old techniques and bring in new creative ways of doing business. They are able to provide services/products that are valued in the emerging markets remote from the mainstream markets.

10.3.1 Involving the Community in the SENO Innovation

The SENOs believe in the co-creation of their activities in the community they are serving. Findings show that they take a deliberate role in actively involving their community in the whole innovation process. For instance, Debora shared that their organization is "a sphere where we involve all stakeholders to provide ideas on how best we can create products that are relevant. We allow our customers to give us feedback on how best we can meet their needs." She further explained that the customers conceive most of their products, saying: "We personally ask them on the types of crafts they are looking for, so that we can make them. The interface with our customers helps in understanding the mind of the customer. So, most of our creative designs come from the customers." Involving customers in the process of innovation promotes customers' loyalty to the SENOs' business and at the same time brings in more customers. John of Hope Inc. expressed his satisfaction in involving the customers in all their innovations, saying, "We understand that our innovation is not only for us, but also makes our customers happy and satisfied. Therefore, we deliberately get feedback and use their thoughts as we continuously improve our services." The SENOs realize the importance of giving stakeholders a voice in the work of the organization. For instance, Peter, the Care Malawi Principal, explained that the idea to run a high school came after massive consultation with the community regarding their needs. They conducted a survey to understand the needs of the community.

It is intriguing to see how the SENOs respond to communities before embarking on any product or service. Stakeholders sometimes get frustrated when they are not put at the center of the activities of the organization. Henry of CYON shared that as an organization, they feel it is important to involve their customer base in responding to their needs as they make other innovations. He said he sends employees out into the community to determine its pressing needs. Then they respond to those needs with innovative responses. Kelvin of CAISD said that competition is intense in today's increasingly changing global market. It is therefore important for the firms to sustain their competitive edge and set themselves apart. Creating client-focused products/services has been essential in SENOs' flourishing. The SENOs create competitive advantage through engaging customers in the product/service planning and implementation process. The research participants argue that to create successful products, the firms are required to change their customer relations through intimate knowledge of the customer, which comes through honest engagement with the clients.

10.4 Chapter Conclusion

The SENOs continually embrace innovation as a central principle for survival and flourishing. Kumar et al. (2020) liken innovation to the biological process of mutation which keeps species abreast in survival race. It is not that any business needs to face constant innovation for its success. The SENOs can improve its profitability and performance of the firm through constant innovation.

Chapter 11
Engaging the External Environment

The social enterprising nonprofit organizations' external environment plays a big role in the operation and the flourishing of the organization. The duality of the SENOs calls for the ability to understand the external environment that affects both the charity and the business entity.

11.1 The Community for Acceptance

Several of the founders highlighted the fact that SENOs and their activities need to be accepted in the community. It is intriguing how community ownership of the SENO promotes the flourishing of the organization. The interviews indicate that social enterprising organizations take their community as an important asset in the success of the organization. Leaders in the SENOs have realized that a good working relationship with the community is pivotal in the operation of the organization. Luke of CDECO pointed out that it becomes difficult to achieve the organization's mission and vision if there is any social gap between the organization and the community. He realized that for the organization to make social impact and profits, it should appeal to the needs of their community. Kelvin of CAISD suggested the same, saying:

> We have the children, the youths and women participating into our programs. We have so many women leaders in the radio listeners' clubs and so many youths as well as children too, producing and presenting programs on the radio. In short, our target audience have become participants in the development, growth and sustainability of the radio station.

This means that earning the community's support to some extent hinges on the leadership's ability to build trust with the entire community they are serving and even beyond. Luke shared an instance when they lost trust from their community that even led to donors losing trust in what they do. They first worked on mending

Z. Chijere, *Nonprofit Social Enterprises*, CSR, Sustainability, Ethics & Governance, https://doi.org/10.1007/978-3-031-60234-4_11

their relationship with the community before they started reinvesting in the organization's activities. He attributes the popularity of their SENO to the good connections they have with the community.

The findings further suggest that being unique helps the SENO to build strong connections with their community. Being unique simply means that the organization provides community-tailored activities or products. Bruce of MSAHI explained that uniqueness serves as the mediator between social exclusion and decision choice by the customers. The flourishing SENO focuses on viewing the community as an asset and creating community-oriented services. Along the same lines, Henry of CYON said that one of the things they do is ensure that they involve the community in their decision-making process. This helps them in producing products that are acceptable to their customer base because they are unique to the community. He said that when doing their charity work, they work on involving all necessary stakeholders. Entities that see value in the customers and involve their constituents perform better in their industries. This sums up the impact that community involvement in development creates, for the flourishing of every entity.

11.2 Adapting to the Country's Political and Economic Environment

Interview findings mostly suggested that economic conditions in the country influence organizations' flourishing. The interviewees remarked that political risk has been high in Malawi, which has affected the economic status of the country. Kelvin (CAISD) explained that "theories have changed, economic environment has changed, the political scenario has changed and many other things." He cites these changes as a main reason why most organizations find it difficult to survive in Malawi. However, he says that if one plays their cards well, it is possible to survive in this environment. The SENOs that are flourishing are able to create strategies that help them to navigate the economic environment, which determines the destination of most organizations. Phillip of CYON described how SENOs in the media sector have been negatively affected by the turmoil caused by the country's economic instability, saying:

> For three months there was political parties' campaign for country's presidency. So the business community was hesitant because we did not know who would win so we could not invest much. Off the elections went. But what followed? We had uneasiness, tension, and demonstrations, so most people were not advertising.

He further lamented:

> Every time there is a drastic economic hustle, the first victim is always the media because lesser adverts are placed. Lesser business is advertised. And largely the media generates income from advertising. So once that is lost then there is hell.

When the economy and the political platform become hard and unstable, the customer base is affected, which leaves them either not buying or looking for lower-quality cheap goods, hence greatly affecting the profitability of the organization. One manager cited an example of the Art Box Inc. products, saying:

> Maybe it is something to do with the financial capacity of Malawians at large, maybe they would rather pay less. They also seem to be well connected with local tailors and so they purchase the fabric themselves and commission something, while as the expatriates are not so well connected, they also appreciate the number of people that are supported through the project and so they are more willing to pay the price to it.

Hope Inc. overcame this by segmenting their customer base. They created products that appeal to a specific high-end group of individuals, including most of the expatriates working in the country. Linda, a Manager at Hope Inc., explained,

> The appeal of Chitenje as a piece of decor is more of a recent thing. It used to be more of clothing. So, it has to do with the target Audience. Lilongwe is great because it has the highest percentage of expatriates, but still more, there is a gap in how much we can sell.

Segmenting the market base has been one of the strategies that has helped several SENOs remain in business. The participants indicated that they are affected by poor economic conditions at the microlevel that broadly affect the buying power of individuals. Linda and her team indicated that the ability to know the economic environment enabled the organizations to plan their approaches. They believe that businesses profit by analyzing the external environment and segmenting their customer base, just as Hope Inc. has done.

In Malawi, like other African countries, politics plays a big role in the success of any organization. Politics affects the economy and how business is done. The founders shared that the political environment in Malawi is unpredictable, which influences how the business is conducted. Flourishing is influenced by these unpredictable changes. Most organizations attributed their failures over the past decade to the instability that the country has been experiencing on the political scene. The study participants highlighted the issues of the taxation system, which they feel has choked their operations. As Luke (CDECO) explained: "The general environment despite it being widely said to be supportive, is not supportive as is it proclaiming outside there, mainly because there are no policies that promotes social enterprises." Participants shared that SENOs also suffer in their operations due to a lack of clear policies regarding investment that might guide their operations and act as their shields. Commenting on this, Luke said:

> I would have loved if there were clear policies in terms of investment in the country as well as ownership of companies even the actual registration because if I am Indian how I do register a company and then that company is Malawian company but that is what is happening in the country. So those are the challenges that we have and ironically the government is even championing the buy Malawi strategy.

Mike of CAISD added:

> On legislation government is not doing its job. We are sleeping on the job as a country. Worse still, the policy framework favors the foreign business. It does not provide a space for social enterprises working with poor people. Right now, it is one size fits all.

However, some SENOs like MSAHI and CYON have directly benefited from the government. One founder explained how closely he works with the government in his projects. He applauded this relationship with the government, as the Government of Malawi has been assisting him with provisions of duty-free status on most imports, and he also does several projects with the government. Similarly, Dave of MSAHI remarked:

> I have graded a road up to 20 kilometers in Dowa and people are using it. I have built a school block at Nkanile Primary School, I also buy blankets which I give to old people in the villages… and I am doing what the government is supposed to be doing. Therefore, they support me when I need them.

This kind of relationship has led nonprofit ventures and even social enterprises to gain more tax waivers and even some individualized support from the government. Dave (MSAHI founder) and Kelvin (CYON founder) extensively discussed the importance of formal and informal ties with political party leaders and governmental officials to the success of businesses. They argued that political ties provide the greatest benefits, as several other founders also suggested. Such ties create strategic benefits that give SENOs regulatory favor and investment resources. These participants explained that ties with government officials also help facilitate both business and social activities in the organization. They stressed that SENOs' relationship with the government is of paramount importance because it fosters some waivers and support from the government.

As vital as it is for SENOs to relate well with the government in their operations, however, one manager observed that it is also critical for the government to competently play its role of providing a conducive environment in which SENOs can operate. This interviewee argued that the government has to legislate good laws that will favor SENOs. Overall, the findings reveal that the main ecosystem challenges facing SENOs are uncertainties in the regulatory framework and the lack of adequate financial and nonfinancial support for social entities. Phillip of CYON suggested that broadcasting equipment like transmitters for nonprofit organizations should be tax-free. He lamented: "There's a heavy tax-- the materials are bought at a lower cost outside, but for them to land in the country you find there's a lot of tax involved." The SENOs in all sectors also felt the pinch of poor government regulations and a taxation system that overlooks waivers for social enterprising nonprofit organizations.

The SENO that is able to analyze the political environment is in a good position to understand major shifts in the economy of the country and is able to make prudent business decisions. The ability to identify risk and opportunity associated with business in the political and economic environment has an impact on business growth. Therefore, the research participants have called upon SENOs to constantly analyze government utterances and actions and then align themselves well with the government. They call on the organizations that are dual in nature to analyze political risks, such as intraparty power games, policy inconsistencies, and political terrorism, if they are to be successful. The SENOs that are able to analyze the political and economic environment are able to grow and survive because they are able to anticipate shifts within the industry induced by the economy. The participants believe that governmental ties commonly create strategic benefits that a firm can use to facilitate business activities. A relationship with dominant government officials provides regulatory benefits that favor the organization. This is exactly what we see in the work of MSAHI and CYON that align themselves with the people in power who support them with many waivers and support from the government in their work.

11.3 Controlling the Supply Chain: Making Raw Materials Available

Managing raw material suppliers is one of the external environment elements that affect the performance and flourishing of the SENO. It is easy for SENOs to survive when they are able to dictate the supply chain. Proper supply chain management procedures and practices influence the performance of the business. There are several strategies and practices that SENOs use in the operational performance of their business.

Several managers indicated that they have built traditional suppliers, which makes it easy for them to dictate the suppliers of the raw material. For instance, Hope Vita Meals (an enterprise under MSAHI) is directly involved in creating the raw material base. The only thing that the enterprise does is support these local farmers in the production process. The ability to have traditional suppliers and control the process has been ideal for many SENOs' success. The participants indicated that having no or little competition in the supply chain industry gives them an ability to focus on the low-price differentiation for their products. In a bid to retain the desired quality in their industry, Tonga Foundation decided to train their own people in hospitality. In order to have minimum competition in finding talent, they invest in having their people trained by professionals from other countries. They hire villagers with no knowledge of the positions they are hired for, and then the organization brings professionals who train the workforce in different work according to their positions. Similarly, CSE has had its team's capacity well built; Bill, the founder of CSE, shared: "We make our own cement blocks, we don't want to use burnt bricks, you might have heard about inter-locking blocks, these are the blocks that are made here, and we use them for building everything. We have got our own team and we make our own blocks because we even have our own machines."

Some SENOs cannot produce their own raw materials. Nevertheless, this study has established that those SENOs that cannot produce their own raw materials are in the forefront in creating strategies that will help them to control the supply chain. The SENOs in this category focus on multiple suppliers, which ensures that they will have the required quality and quantity of raw materials. One such SENO is Hope Inc., which relies on women who get materials from Tanzania or Zambia. However, its founder lamented that sometimes the materials come without colors, and it is often difficult to get the type of cloth they want. They want to control the industry by buying a cloth-making machine that will guarantee the availability of the cloth they look for. Linda explained: "When you produce your own raw materials, you are in control of your product from start to finish because at the moment we are confined to what fabrics someone is designing or importing." On this issue, Luke shared that firms need to understand their suppliers if they are to be successful in the supply chain industry. He further argues that corroborative and customized partnership with the suppliers is key in the success of any enterprise. The SENOs see the need for enterprise resource planning that will help to develop suppliers, which becomes key in the success of the enterprise.

11.3.1 Dealing with Sector Rivalry

Securing a market position gives a business a reasonable chance of success. The ability to compete in the industry is an important element for success. Many organizations cease to exist due to their failure to make their mark. Therefore, the ability to beat rivals in the industry has been an essential element in the success of SENOs. The research participants in this study indicated that knowing and understanding competitors is the critical step in survival. They believe that the long-term prosperity of the organizations comes from both resilience to competition and the ability to exist in a symbiotic state. Resilience is needed by the organizations to cope with turbulent external environments, ranging from smaller agitations to high-impact events.

The founders in this study strategically choose strategies that will make their products unique to overcome competition from other organizations. Organizations that are flourishing tap into a unique industry, which is hard for other organizations to imitate. For instance, the Tonga Foundation entered a unique hospitality industry. The founder shared that their lodge is a holiday resort, not just any other lodge. This is a unique approach, since there are not many holiday resorts in Malawi. Levi of Tonga Foundation explained: "When it comes to eco-friendly hotels, we are the only one in Malawi. We are in the high-end wilderness lodge business where we have received several awards as being one of the best in Africa, not just in Malawi." Although there may be competition from other hospitality organizations, Tonga's uniqueness is in the holiday resort aspect. It is the same with CYON, which ventured into the media industry. This is an industry into which few businesses think of venturing, due to the scale of investment that is required to start this business; very few are able to enter these markets.

Several other managers, however, face competition from substitute unbranded products. Hope Inc., which has ventured into the craft industry, said that they face stiff competition from a thousand unbranded craftsmen working in town. The market in Malawi, just like other developing countries, is saturated with counterfeit products. SENOs deplore the lack of control in the market that hinders the growth of business. Their solution is to rely on the international market that they are currently developing. Debora of Hope Inc. said: "The unbranded competition is also a reason we export crafts because that won't happen on international market. We are opening a shop at the airport, and we are also developing our online shop." She further explained that the Malawi market is limited; the vast majority of their customers are expatriate residents and some from the upper middle class. They have almost finished incorporating an American organization that will act as a distributor, and then they will open a simple online shop as well as storage for a large number of things, initially once a year and then twice and even three times a year. They are desperate for a bigger market, and they also want to open a shop at the airport again to catch tourists who may not know about their shop in town.

The research participants reported that competitive intelligence improves the market performance for businesses. The action of gathering, analyzing, and distributing intelligence about the business and its competitors helps to support the enterprise in creating strategies. The founders indicated that the ability to make forward-looking decisions through competitive intelligence helps them be market leaders. Mike of CAISD agreed, stating that competitive intelligence helps the firm to achieve effectiveness and efficiency in the marketplace. The enterprises that fail to adapt to competition risk fading away. The ability to adapt to the environment helps SENOs beat the competition, since it helps generate customer value through speedy delivery of products and services at the convenience of the customers.

The research participants also explained that at times they have huge competition from large international enterprises. Since Malawi's market is liberalized, foreign investors have an upper hand in doing trade. Thomas of Hope Inc. lamented that they face stiff competition with international enterprises that want to engage in the same activities that Hope sponsors. These international firms have an upper hand in terms of knowledge, resources, and support from donors as compared to local social enterprises. At the same time, since Malawi does not have clear policies that protect the interests of social enterprising nonprofit organizations, SENOs' operations and consequently the profit margins are affected. Nevertheless, although competition from large international enterprises hinders the growth of local SENOs, the participants shared that their SENOs focus on their core competencies to appeal to their constituents. At the same time, they have called on the government to set regulations that will support SENOs' survival and growth. The SENOs see the need for the government to set and abide by investment policies that will help the country's indigenous SENOs.

Being innovative has been central in dealing with competition in their industry according to this research project. This is supported in the literature. Medlin and Ellegaard (2015) name competition as the driving force for innovation in many industries. The SENOs investigated in this study have indicated that competition has provoked innovation in their competitive processes. This competitive intensity has resulted in many SENOs finding creative ways to make their products/services unique, with many focusing on the quality of their products coupled with best branding.

11.3.2 Developing the Enabling Environment

SENOs studied in this project all call for an enabling environment from the government and other stakeholders in order to be successful. The International Labor Organization reports that sustainable organizations do not and cannot exist in a vacuum. All organizations operate within a political, social, and economic context and are subject to regulatory and institutional constraints. The research participants agreed that without an enabling environment, SENOs cannot produce optimal results. They focus their discussion on the government's desire to create an environment that is suitable for the growth of SENOs. According to Levi of CDECO, the major problem is that the SENOs are treated like any other business venture without regard to the fact that their profits are reinvested into the community through charity work. He cited an example of the enterprise they run for which they pay too many fees and taxes that at times hinder their operation as an organization. He explained, "There is Value Added Tax, there is Tourism Levy, and I have to pay them all. As if that is not enough, they also charge several other fees. So, when all these are put together to the customers, they find our services very expensive."

In a bid to level the operating surface and create a conducive environment from the government, Linda of Hope Inc. unveiled their planned means to get the challenges fixed:

> We are preparing ourselves to start a conversation on how we can get tax breaks so that we can easily ship things and get materials. I mean we try our best to buy most of the materials locally but sometimes they are not available. The serious conversation that we are working on is to approach government to give us the freedom to do business so that we are recognized. They should also consider giving us the freedom of getting the raw materials without paying the overall taxes. After all, it is the community that benefit from the profits of the organization.

Many founders interviewed in this study call for a better investment policy that will benefit the companies that focus on community development. The founders doubt there is currently an investment policy in existence that would protect and guide SENOs that focus on community development. Luke of CDECO stated it like this:

> Maybe there is a policy, but in terms of implementation it is lacking. Another area where we feel to be important, is on the returns that the government expects from us through the taxes. We are not given the chance to grow. The moment they see you ticking, they pounce on you. Instead of being supportive they just want to get from us and there is no room for discussion.

Others complained that the government as regards implementation does not support the few policies available for the business sector. Mike of CAISD remarked, "The challenges that we have…ironically, they (the government) are even championing the buy Malawi strategy. That just sounds a good theory but practically such initiatives are not being implemented." Several managers feel that the Government of Malawi fails to protect social enterprising nonprofit organizations but instead has policies that favor foreign investments compared to indigenous ones. It is the view of the SENOs in this study that the general investment environment, despite being widely said to be neutral, practically is not as supportive as is claimed. SENOs lament that their growth is hindered by the government's inability to create a conducive environment for them to thrive. Investment policy in Africa lacks the power to serve local investors, especially those businesses run by nonprofit organizations.

11.4 Chapter Conclusion

The social enterprise's external environment plays a big role in the operation and the flourishing of the SENOs. Leaders of flourishing SENOs show that they have a good grasp of the external environment, and this has a huge impact in their success. Adapting to the external environment has been key in the flourishing of the organizations. Both the charity and the business parts of SENOs seek to be relevant by adapting to whatever is happening around them. This chapter discussed how the SENOs approach government regulations, community ownership, the political environment, the perceived government support, and the competition with other companies in the industry.

Chapter 12
Market Leadership

Market leadership is basically the position an organization has in the industry by having either a monopoly of market share or profitability margin. Being preeminent in the market and thus being a dominant player in the industry have been a central strategy for many organizations. These organizations see market leadership as being the first movers in the industry in terms of technology or products/services introduced. Leadership in the market must be viewed both from the lens of the nonprofit and that of the for-profit entity in the SENO. This section analyzes market leadership as a tool for flourishing SENOs.

To flourish, SENOs focus on gaining a dominant market position, which will give them a strategic advantage over other organizations. The findings from this study suggest that most thriving SENOs have a good market share in their industry. For instance, Luke posits that success belongs to organizations that are able to secure a market position and gain dominance. In today's market, competition is intense; therefore, it is important for organizations to ascertain how their products or services can sustain an edge and set themselves apart. An organization's relative position determines whether its performance and profitability are above or below the industry average. For flourishing, a sustainable competitive advantage is determined by the above average performance of the SENOs' activities. The findings suggest that the ability to control the behavior of the market has been an essential element in the success of these organizations. The organizations in this study are focused on finding a unique market position in their industry. The three major issues raised by study participants concerning market leadership were creating products and/or services of high quality, ability to deal with substitute products/services, and selecting a customer base and unique business niche.

Z. Chijere, *Nonprofit Social Enterprises*, CSR, Sustainability, Ethics & Governance, https://doi.org/10.1007/978-3-031-60234-4_12

12.1 Creating Products and/or Services of High Quality

The findings show that successful SENOs focus on product/service differentiation in order to outbid others in the market. The interviewees put effort into making sure that their products are of high quality compared to what others are providing on the market. They realize the need to focus on being the trendsetters in the industry for the products/services they are providing. The Creative Director for the Art Box Ltd., a Hope Inc. enterprise, indicated that quality is paramount in their work. She pointed out that their craft is different from what other artisans provide in the city. They deliberately take time to innovate in order to have products that are appealing to their customers. She says that that even though the price of their products might be higher than that of their competitors, their appeal to quality should not be compromised. She extensively discussed the importance of integrating six sigma into business strategy. Six sigma is a complex process of improvement that focuses on improving quality performance. This helps firms to thrive and to achieve a negligible number of defects, corresponding to the probability associated with market standards. Six sigma is the attempt to relegate defects and quality problems to the very tail of distribution. Making such problems rare exceptions has been key to many SENOs, helping SENOs like Hope Inc. to focus on products that are above standard quality.

As discussed in the previous chapter, the founders strategically invest in their workforce in order to create products that are above standard. The SENOs emphasize that quality rests within an empowered workforce. For instance, Mtendere Vital Meals, a social enterprise under MSAHI, reported that they make sure that they send their staff for training in order to create quality products. The Manager for the Mtendere Vital Meals said that every year they send individuals to different training institutions where they gain knowledge, abilities, and skills for their work. This is the same with Tonga Foundation, whose director explained: "We exposed our workforce to trainings by international experts like chefs and experts in hospitality. This has made them be able to prepare great food and being the best tour guides in Malawi." These two organizations realize the importance of having a workforce that has knowledge, ability, and skills in the production of the services/products. They make sure that they do detailed packaging. They believe that quality of the products is the center of the organizations; therefore, they need to have well trained personnel to produce quality products/services.

Dave, the founder of MSAHI, also believes that increasing production quality helps the firm to deliver maximum value at the least possible cost. The research participants see the need for investing in the organization's workforce in order to make unique and high-quality products. Quality products and level of differentiation depend on how much the managers are willing to invest in making sure that they constantly innovate.

12.1.1 Creating Unique Products/Services

Beyond quality, SENOs also focus on creating a unique product that becomes difficult to imitate by competitors by focusing on high-end customers. Titus of Tonga said: "Our uniqueness is the fact that you will find our place very relaxing. You just go there find tranquility and the peace that you will enjoy." He indicated that their approach to creating a relaxing environment cannot be easily imitated by their competitors because they invest a lot in being unique and different. He further indicated the long-term desire of the enterprise to be different from other dual-mission organizations that are doing the same. However, Debora, the project manager at Hope Inc., sees that the zeal is to make every product according to the design with high-end quality checks, so that people don't just buy the material because they were made by refugees but because they are worth the money. Hope Inc. products are not cheap if you compare them to their products here in Lilongwe, but people still buy them because they are unique.

Quality and unique products help in increasing sales according to study participants. Bill of CSE indicated that to produce unique and quality services calls for intensive resource mobilization and capital injections, issues like transmitters to gain widespread coverage. This is linked to the loyalty that the SENOs enjoy based on the quality of their products and services. William, the RMM School Principal, indicated that the growth of their school is attributed to it being different from others in the market. He said that beyond the profits, the school focuses on making a difference to the students. Since the community knows the school focuses on quality in the teaching and learning process, they have more students than their competitors. The school started with 6 students 7 years ago, and now they have over 400 students.

The study also uncovered the fact that the quality of the products minimizes threats to SENOs' performance. Participants indicated that since their products cannot be easily substituted, they have control of the market. Henry indicates that threats in sales are not really challenging because their product is unique. Competitors cannot imitate their products or try to make something similar because they are in an industry that is not saturated by products. He explained: "Currently we are the only company producing high nutritious flour and we have customers that know us. We have created relationships with customers and so it's just keeping our customers happy that works for us, on the production side." He urged organizations to create products of high customer satisfaction for the business to survive. Other interviewees mentioned that a set of effective quality control performance and improvement models needs to be established for success in creating products that are above standards. The SENOs indicated that customer satisfaction and business profit can be achieved by creating product quality and service value through timely and effective promotion of product design, manufacturing, and service quality.

12.2 Selecting Customer Base

Customers play an important role in the strategic operation of a SENO. Study participants believe that creating successful services requires a change in customer relationship and approach. They shared the need for indigenous enterprises to focus on developing a deep understanding and an intimate knowledge of their customers. This calls for understanding how to select a customer base and knowing how to engage those customers. The SENOs indicated that they work on increasing market share and at the same time having a satisfied customer base.

Successful SENOs have a clear targeted market for their products and services. Kelvin of CYON shared that their organization strategically chooses their targeted customers and provides uniquely tailored products and services to this unique customer base. He says that, as an enterprise, they are proud to be able to tell everyone that they target the youth, women, and children. Their programming and approach to the radio station focuses on keeping this customer base happy and satisfied. He explained: "Apparently most men say, where are we? It should be noted that men are not left out, but they are our secondary audience. Our main audience are youths, women and children." Commenting on creating a unique customer base, CAISD Executive Director explained: "All our companies and activities focuses on how we can meet the local farmers with a modern approach of agriculture. So, our targeted customers are the local farmers." The organization has a unique target audience and works on satisfying their constituents. They realize how important it is to have a segmented customer base.

While having a unique customer base is important, findings suggest that most SENOs in this study include their customers in the strategic operation of the organization. The Creative Director at Hope Inc. indicated that they include customers when they are coming up with a new product or strategy. She said they get feedback from customers during the execution and design of the product. This helps them to come up with a product that will reach the satisfaction of their customers. If there is a social gap between the organization and the community, it becomes difficult to achieve these goals. The SENO believes that to grow, they must depend exclusively on the community accepting them and their products and services. So, they have targeted customers, but at the same time they also work on engaging them in major decisions made as a school. The SENO founders indicated that involving customers in their activities facilitates the acceptability of such products or services. This helps in making products that are focused and tailored to the customers' needs. Phillip of CYON pointed out that for them to win customers' trust, they need to engage with all stakeholders in the enterprise. As Phillip put it:

> The advertisers want to see the real product. They want visible audience on your radio and that is attained when we can hear or feel the audience being involved either through recorded program, live programs or through any other means that can feature on radio. I may not go in details on that, but once that is attained, the marketing community will know. That is the reason this station commands a particular audience.

Phillip talked about the need for SENOs to be in close working relationships with the customer:

> If you are targeting a particular audience and that audience is not participative into the program that you have set up, then you are already on your way to failure. That is the reason that prompts us involve our clients to express their needs and then we make products to meet those needs. Such are the things I can attribute to our success.

The study participants are willing to pay the costs of involving customers, since they know that it will help provide services that meet the needs of their customers. To appeal to the customers' taste, the SENOs see the need of speaking to their customers in a language they will understand. This comes at an additional cost, since they have to go the extra mile just to get more community involvement. However, it pays a lot of dividends to the success of the organization.

12.3 Unique Business Niche

Findings from the interviews show that SENOs work hard in establishing a unique business niche. The SENOs indicated that they are market-focused rather than going with popular business trends. Research participants indicated that they don't just copy what others are doing, but they also intentionally study the market they want to invest in and create a unique business approach. William explained that selecting a business niche is vital in the successful operation of the business. The success of many enterprises originates from their ability to not only select a business that is unique but also choose a market that will correspond with their charity work. The SENOs reject an unfocused one-size-fits-all approach in favor of a well-tailored target.

When discussing the market base, one manager indicated that their organization targets high-end customers in whom most Malawians businesses rarely invest; the organization relies on international customers because most Malawians cannot afford their services. That uniqueness is why it still occupies a first position in Malawi and Africa. The research participants said that they all work on identifying themselves as a unique business rather than hopping from one business to another. Mike of CAISD explained how they identified their market niche. He said, "We are irrigation experts because we actually realize that irrigation is a catalyst that will be used to address any problem that may rise." He explained that they would not move from irrigation: "It as an industry that is not saturated by products but at the same time irrigation is our trademark. People identify us with irrigation and agriculture technologies, and we cannot wake up today and say we are opening a transport company."

As an organization producing high irrigation experts, he continued, they promote irrigation and food security, so they are in that business no matter what challenges they may come across. Still, in terms of the connotation of market niche, Kelvin of CYON shared that they are a company producing high sexual and reproductive health products simply because this is where there is a business mandate. Unique industries deliberately drive out other potential market entrants because of the costs of setting up the business. Most industries into which SENOs venture require heavy investments that other enterprises cannot manage. For instance, running a national radio station is not cheap in Malawi, which reduces competition in the industry. Explaining their uniqueness in the market niche, Bill of CSE elaborates:

> Currently we are doing digital services for a company in the U.K and another company in the U.S, in dollars and in pounds and we have got a team working on that. When you look at our bundle per week here of internet you will be shocked; we take more than the banks because we have got to be live all the time with those companies we are working with, and they told us that if we are not online, we should forget about the business with them. There are only a few companies which are doing that, so we are trying as much as possible to look at enterprises; some are born from outside Malawi through our colleagues whilst some of them are generated here.

Sharing their approach, John of CYON added:

> We noted that agricultural financing is risky. That's why most people don't want it, but we still have framed much of our products to address many of those risks. Instead of us giving people the money to buy for themselves, we use our own department to install everything for them…and then the agri-business comes in and will take an agreement with the people.

SENOs see the benefits of going into an industry that is unique and not saturated by many other enterprises. They are willing to invest in order to become leaders in the industry. Levi, who operates an eco-lodge, indicated that there are few companies that are interested in this industry. Because of the nature of the business, their SENO faces less competition because they are one of a few.

12.3.1 Dealing with Substitute Products/Services

The ability to deal with substitute products has been a key factor to some SENOs in dealing with competition and staying in business. The participants indicated that they focus on innovation and quality of the products as one means of overcoming this challenge. The SENOs focus on investing capital innovatively to beat the substitute products as well as expanding their customer base to international markets as a solution to the competition. In addition, some SENOs indicated that their attitude toward customers has helped them in terms of customer loyalty and expansion of their customer base. Most SENOs believe that keeping customers happy promotes their products and services. The SENOs look at customers' loyalty as the center of their competitive advantage, and thus they invest in creating a good working relationship with the customers. Phillip admitted that it is not cheap or easy to sustain a media house like a radio station. Just like a TV station or newspaper, their biggest challenge is that if they take an audience for granted, they will eventually lose them.

The research participants discussed the need for businesses to be quick in delivering products or services if they want to be relevant on the market. Dave, founder of [name of Seno], shared that, as a SENO, one thing they focus on is speed in implementation of their business processes:

> We know we have targets, and we focus on delivering our product the quickest possible without much waste in the process. Meeting the targets and datelines has been one of the areas we have mentored ourselves. This places the business ahead of our competitors.

Speed in implementation reduces waste, and organizations are thus better able to utilize human capital. Porter (1980, 2008) elaborated on the concept of competitive advantage for businesses. He outlined three generic competitive strategies—low price, focus, and differentiation—as core principles for business success. Low price competitive strategies focus on providing the lowest price compared to the others in the same industry. The focus strategy involves having a specific niche of industry or programs. The differentiation strategy focuses on the organization providing something unique and distinct compared to what others are providing.

This study has revealed that the SENOs investigated mainly focused on differentiation for their competitive advantage. Most of the products or services offered are more expensive as compared to others on the market. However, their ability to focus on a market segment and to provide high-quality products has helped them stay competitive. It should be noted that consumers are continually faced with new buying decisions; therefore, market leadership and "pioneership" have been central to many SENOs. The study participants also stressed the importance of creating competitive advantage through human resources. They see the need for HR practices that build and support resources critical to competitive advantage. Such a competitive advantage through HR is difficult to imitate and helps the SENOs to flourish in their industry.

12.4 Chapter Conclusion

Market leadership also emerged as a flourishing factor. Due to the double bottom-line nature of SENOs, they need a blended approach of all three concerns to flourish. Organizations that are able to innovate continue to remain relevant in the environment they are operating. The organizations help the workforce to be innovative by training the employees on the important operational issues of the organizations. They allow their workforce to try out their ideas, a practice which is essential if the workforce is to feel closely connected to the organization. Flourishing organizations are those that invest in innovation. The organizations also aim for market leadership by focusing on the quality of their products/services.

Chapter 13
In Closing

This study focused on understanding the concept of flourishing in indigenous non-profit social enterprises working in the educational and human services sectors in sub-Saharan Africa. The study followed Charmaz's constructivist grounded theory, which has its foundations in relativism (Charmaz, 2007; Bryant & Charmaz, 2007; Charmaz, 1983). The grounded theory approach appreciates the multiple truths and realities of subjectivism as one tries to understand the lived experiences of the study participants. I studied 23 SENOs located across sub-Saharan Africa. All these SENOs were founded and are operated by indigenous Africans. The fundamental concern was to identify factors that led to these organizations flourishing, which I believe has contributed to their survival.

To understand flourishing, I based my discussion on both Aristotle's discourse on flourishing and the modern approach of flourishing which rests in the work of MacIntyre, Seligman, and other scholars of positive psychology and positive organization behavior. Two central concepts in their scholarly works are hedonic well-being and eudaimonic well-being. These terms help us understanding individuals' flourishing. I contend that organizations that focus on enabling individuals in their workforce to flourish both in hedonic and eudaimonic contexts enable these individuals to carry out their responsibilities joyfully, leading to the organization flourishing.

Eight major themes emerged as contributors to SENO flourishing: leadership, governance, human resource management, organizational culture, management of operations in the organization, innovation, market leadership, and management of the external environment. A critical analysis of the influence of these eight factors shows that five of them (leadership, governance, organizational culture, human resource management, and management) strongly influenced SENO flourishing through hedonic well-being as well as eudaimonic well-being, with leadership playing a much stronger critical role in SENOs' flourishing. I have labeled these internal factors since they are influencing the organization from within. They influence the internal organizational climate that spurs hedonic and eudaimonic well-being. I term the other three factors (market leadership, innovation, and managing the

Z. Chijere, *Nonprofit Social Enterprises*, CSR, Sustainability, Ethics & Governance, https://doi.org/10.1007/978-3-031-60234-4_13

external environment) external factors. These are oriented to issues having to do with the external environment. They have strong influence on eudaimonic well-being but just weak influence on hedonic well-being. All these factors influence each other.

SENOs' flourishing springs from a combination of the organization's hedonic well-being and eudaimonic well-being. To flourish, organizations need to create a strong symbiotic relationship between hedonic and eudaimonic well-beings. SENOs that have dual missions (the charity and the for-profit sides) need to balance the tension between the different sides of their mission. Such organizations need checks in the operation of the charity and the business sides.

Contextually, this study has indicated that SENO flourishing is a multidimensional issue that encompasses several factors feeding into both hedonic and eudaimonic well-beings. The hedonic focus provides an internal organizational climate that creates a satisfying environment for the workforce. The internal organizational climate plays a vital role in creating a happy working environment. This inspires the workforce into creativity and into innovative and positive organizational citizenship behavior which becomes essential in the attainment of goals by the dual-mission organizations. On the other hand, the eudaimonic well-being enables the organization to function well. The study indicates that flourishing happens when an organization is healthy in both dimensions. Organizational health brings about pleasure and wholesomeness in members of its workforce as they identify with the organization and work toward achieving intended organizational goals.

13.1 The Lessons

The SENOs in this study provide a powerful model for those running or intending to run an organization combining social enterprising and nonprofit activities. Many attributes have been identified that provide a framework for success and flourishing for social enterprising nonprofit organizations operating in the health and educational as well as agricultural services in Malawi, which, I would contend, are applicable in other developing countries. The theoretical model of flourishing in this study offers a vital tool for running organizations, especially SENOs. Ensuring attention to the factors provides a SENO some advantage over their competitors and will help many SENOs in their dual missions.

Duality of mission is a source of tension that, if not properly managed, can bring the nonprofit down and move the business into liquidation. Cultivating a sense of both hedonic and eudaimonic well-being in the workforce helps in translating vision and mission into action. Leaders' ability to create a framework that prevents the SENOs from drifting away from their mission has been central to the success and subsequent flourishing of their organizations. Such leaders create an environment for innovation, which is crucial to the success of the product/service that the SENO is providing. At the same time, it calls for leadership that is able to sense the need for inspiring and engaging employees to joyfully invest their energy in the organization. One-way leaders do this is rotating directorship of a SENO, thus bringing about leadership diversity, significant encouragement to the workforce, and the needed renewal every 2 years.

Organizational culture is another fundamental factor that drives SENOs' flourishing. SENOs will benefit from developing clear, well-defined relational values and beliefs based on virtues. These in turn develop an organizational climate that inspires innovation and the resulting commitment from the workforce to engage in meaningful innovation at all levels. This extends to HR concerns. The need here is for clear hiring, and motivation procedures in order to retain talents have been central to the success and subsequent flourishing of many SENOs.

Market leadership through unique products/services differentiates flourishing SENOs from those that are languishing. The flourishing SENOs focus on meeting industry standards coupled with innovative market leadership strategies. The need for innovation and investment in organizational experiments cannot be undervalued in flourishing organizations.

13.2 Closing Thoughts

The findings in this study provide insight into the survival and subsequent flourishing of SENOs in Malawi. Even with my professional experience in running a SENO, developing the profiles of the leaders and managers in this study has given me a new perspective on running successful SENOs. The founders, directors, and managers in the SENOs I studied have indispensable knowledge of the running of these nonprofit social enterprises. The rigor of grounded theory research helped me to understand and learn from the experiences of these successful leaders and managers in the field of social enterprising and nonprofits.

References

Abdioglu, N., Khurshed, A., & Stathopoulos, K. (2015). Firm innovation and institutional investment: The role of the Sarbanes–Oxley Act. *The European Journal of Finance, 21*(1), 71–92.

Acuto, M. (2010). Global cities: Gorillas in our midst. *Alternatives, 35*(4), 425–448. https://doi.org/10.1177/030437541003500405

Ahmed, R. (2003). Intellectual capital and firm performance of US multinational firms: A study of the resource-based and stakeholder views. *Journal of Intellectual Capital, 4*(2), 215–226.

Ahmetoglu, G., Akhtar, R., Tsivrikos, D., & Chamorro-Premuzic, T. (2018). The entrepreneurial organization: The effects of organizational culture on innovation output. *Consulting Psychology Journal: Practice and Research, 70*(4), 318–338.

Alfakhri, S. (2018). *Brand management: Co-creating meaningful brands*. Palgrave Macmillan.

Allen, R., & Sims, S. (2018). *The Teacher Gap*. Routledge.

Alter, A. (2000). *The art of relevance*. ABC-CLIO.

Alter, K. (2004). Social enterprise typology. http://www.virtueventures.com/setypology/index.php

Amrhein, L. (2004). The importance of situation and action models for life in old age. In S. Blüher & M. Stosberg (Eds.), *New forms of socialization of age(s) and society* (pp. 59–86). VS Verlag für Sozialwissenschaften.

Anderson, E. (2015). The business enterprise as an ethical agent. In S. Rangan (Ed.), *Performance and progress: Essay on capitalism, business and society* (pp. 435–461). Oxford University Press.

Anirbanc, I. (2019). *PESTEL analysis: Making prudent business decisions for an oil and gas company*. Infiniti Research. https://www.infinitiresearch.com/casestudy/pestel-analysis-oil-and-gas-industry

Arasti, Z., Zandi, F., & Talebi, K. (2014). *Entrepreneurship ecosystem in Iran*. Springer.

Aristotle. (1984). The complete works of Aristotle: The revised Oxford translation. In J. Barnes (Ed.). Princeton University Press. (Original work published 350 B.C.E.).

Aristotle. (1995). *Nicomachean ethics* (T. Irwin, Trans.). Hackett Publishing Company. (Original work published 350 B.C.E.)

Aristotle. (1996a). *The politics and the constitution of Athens* (S. Everson, Trans.). Cambridge University Press.

Aristotle. (1996b). *The Athenian constitution, the Eudemian ethics, on virtues and vices* (H. Rackham, Trans.). Harvard University Press.

Aristotle. (1997) *The politics of Aristotle* (P. Simpson, Trans.). University of North Carolina Press.

Aristotle. (2000). *Nicomachean ethics* (R. Crisp, Trans.). Cambridge University Press.

Arthur, M. B., & Kram, K. E. (1985). Mentoring at work: Developmental relationships in organizational life. *Administrative Science Quarterly, 3*, 321–341.

Z. Chijere, *Nonprofit Social Enterprises*, CSR, Sustainability, Ethics & Governance, https://doi.org/10.1007/978-3-031-60234-4

Audretsch, D. B., Lehmann, E. E., & Schenkenhofer, J. (2020a). *Sustainable rice straw management*. Springer.

Audretsch, D. B., Lehmann, E. E., Meoli, M., & Vismara, S. (2020b). *University evolution, entrepreneurial activity and regional competitiveness*. Springer.

Babbie, E. R. (2007). *The practice of social research*. Thomson Wadsworth.

Badenhorst-Weiss, J. A., & Cilliers, J. O. (2019). Competitive advantage of independent small businesses in Soweto. *Southern African Business Review, 18*(3), 1–21.

Baker, C. (2015). *Foundations of bilingual education and bilingualism*. Multilingual Matters.

Bandura, A. (1994). Self-efficacy. In V. S. Ramachaudran (Ed.), *Encyclopedia of human behavior* (Vol. 4, pp. 71–81). Academic Press. (Reprinted in H. Friedman (Ed.) (1998). *Encyclopediaof mental health*. Academic Press).

Bandura, A. (1998). Personal and collective efficacy in human adaptation and change. In J. G. Adair, D. Belanger, & K. L. Dion (Eds.), *Advances in psychological science, vol. 1* (Personal, social and cultural aspects) (pp. 51–71). Psychology Press.

Banzato, C. R., & Sierra, J. C. V. (2016). Implications of theory and research on strategic leadership: A critical review. *Revista Ibero-Americana De Estratégia, 15*(3), 119–131.

Barman, E. (2008). With strings attached: Nonprofits and the adoption of donor choice. *Nonprofit and Voluntary Sector Quarterly, 37*(1), 39–56.

Bass, B. M. (1985). *Leadership and performance beyond expectations*. Free Press.

Bass, B. M. (1996). *A new paradigm of leadership: An inquiry into transformational leadership*. U.S. Army Research Institute for the Behavioral and Social Sciences.

Bass, B. M. (1999). Two decades of research and development in transformational leadership. *European Journal of Work and Organizational Psychology, 8*(1), 9–32.

Bass, B. M., & Steidlmeier, P. (1999). Ethics, character, and authentic transformational leadership behavior. *The Leadership Quarterly, 10*(2), 181–217.

Battilana, J., Besharov, M. L., & Mitzinneck, B. (2017). On hybrids and hybrid organizing: A review and roadmap for future research. In R. Greenwood, C. Oliver, T. B. Lawrence, & R. E. Meyer (Eds.), *The SAGE handbook of organizational institutionalism* (pp. 128–162). SAGE Publications.

Becchetti, L., & Borzaga, C. (2010). *The economics of social responsibility: The world of social enterprises*. Routledge.

Becchetti, I., Castriota, S., & Tortia, E. C. (2009). Productivity, wages and intrinsic motivations. *Small Business Economics, 41*, 379–399.

Beerel, A. (2009). *Leadership and change management*. SAGE.

Bentham, J. (1954). *Jeremy Bentham's economic writings*. The Royal Economic Society and George Allen & Unwin.

Bhamra, R., Dani, S., & Burnard, K. (2011). Resilience: The concept, a literature review and future directions. *International Journal of Production Research, 49*(18), 5375–5393.

Biddulph, S. (2018). Democratic centralism and administration in China. In F. Hualing, J. Gillespie, P. Nicholson, & W. Partlett (Eds.), *Socialist law in socialist East Asia, socialist law in socialist East Asia, (vol. 1)* (pp. 195–223). Cambridge University Press.

Bielskis, A., & Mardosas, E. (2014). Human flourishing in the philosophical work of Alasdair MacIntyre. *International Journal of Philosophy and Theology, 2*(2), 185–201.

Bilgin, Y., Bilgin, G., & Kilinc, I. (2017). Strategic leadership in civil society organizations: A research on Turkish charities performing international operations. *International Journal of Voluntary and Nonprofit Organizations, 28*(2), 839–863.

Blackburn, R., & Ram, M. (2006). Fix or fixation? The contributions and limitations of entrepreneurship and small firms to combating social exclusion. *Entrepreneurship & Regional Development, 18*(1), 73–89.

Blount, J., & Nunley, P. (2015). Social enterprise, corporate objectives, and the corporate governance narrative. *American Business Law Journal, 52*(2), 201–254.

Bolman, L. G., & Deal, T. E. (2017). *Reframing organizations: Artistry, choice, and leadership* (6th ed.). Jossey-Bass.

Borji, A. (2020). *Defining and measuring financial literacy*. RAND Corporation.

Bornstein, D. (2007). *How to change the world: Social entrepreneurs and the power of new ideas* (Updated ed.). Oxford University Press.
Bornstein, D., Davidson, K., & Vickers, I. (2016). *Social entrepreneurship: What everyone needs to know*. Oxford University Press.
Borzaga, C., & Defourny, J. (2001). *The emergence of social enterprise*. Routledge.
Borzaga, C., Depedri, S., & Tortia, E. (2009). The role of cooperative and social enterprises: A multifaceted approach for an economic pluralism. *IO: Firm Structure*. https://doi.org/10.2139/ssrn.1622143
Bowen, E. R. (1953). *The cooperative road to abundance: The alternative to monopolism and communism*. H. Schuman.
Bowen, D. E., & Ostroff, C. (2004). Understanding HRM-firm performance linkages: The role of the "strength" of the HRM system. *The Academy of Management Review, 29*(2), 203.
Bozkurt, S., & Gligor, D. (2019). Scarcity (versus popularity) cues for rejected customers: The impact of social exclusion on cue types through need for uniqueness. *Journal of Business Research, 99*, 275–281.
Bradshaw, P. (2009). A contingency approach to nonprofit governance. *Nonprofit Management and Leadership, 20*(1), 61–81.
Bressler, M. S. (2012). How small businesses master the art of competition through superior competitive advantage. *Journal of Management and Marketing Research, 11*, 2–9.
Brimhall, K. C. (2019). Inclusion and commitment as key pathways between leadership and nonprofit performance. *Nonprofit Management and Leadership, 30*, 31–49.
Briscoe, R., & Ward, M. (2000). *Helping ourselves: Success stories in cooperative business and social enterprise*. Oak Tree Press.
Brolis, O., & Nyssens, M. (2019). Does the mission of an organization affect the quality of low-skilled jobs in quasi-markets?: A comparison between social enterprises and for-profit organizations. *Voluntas: International Journal of Voluntary and Nonprofit Organizations*. https://doi.org/10.1007/s11266-019-00164-x
Brown, W. A. (2003). Inclusive governance practices in nonprofit organizations and implications for practice. *Nonprofit Management & Leadership, 12*(4), 369–385.
Bruni-Bossio, V., & Willness, C. (2016). The "Kobayashi Maru" meeting: High-fidelity experiential learning. *Journal of Management Education, 40*(5), 619–647.
Bryant, A., & Charmaz, K. (2007). *The SAGE handbook of grounded theory*. SAGE.
Bryant, A., & Charmaz, K. (2007). Grounded theory in historical perspective: An epistemological account. In A. Bryant & K. Charmaz (Eds.), *The SAGE handbook of grounded theory* (pp. 31–57). Sage.
Bukhini, D., Smith, J., & Lewis, K. (2014). *Creating digital stories: EFL learners' engagement, cognitive and metacognitive skills*. JSTOR.
Bunzli, F. (2019). *Sustainable development and social responsibility*. Springer.
Burde, D., Kapit, A., Wahl, R., Guven, O., & Skarpeteig, M. I. (2017a). *Education in emergencies: A review of theory and research*. Springer.
Burde, D., Middleton, J., & Samman, E. (2017b). *Education and conflict: Complexities and prospects for peace*. Oxford University Press.
Burde, D., Kapit, A., Middleton, J. A., & Wahl, R. (2017c). Education in emergencies: A review of theory and research. *Review of Educational Research, 87*(3), 619–658.
Burns, J. M. (2010). *Leadership*. Harper Perennial.
Cain, S., Dobkins, K., & Vul, E. (2016). Texture properties bias ensemble size judgments. *Journal of Vision, 16*(12), 54.
Calabrese, A., & Costa, R. (2015). Strategic thinking and business innovation: Abduction as cognitive element of leaders' strategizing. *Journal of Engineering and Technology Management, 38*, 24–36.
Caldwell, S. D., Herold, D. M., & Fedor, D. B. (2004). Towards an understanding of the relationships between organizational change, individual differences, and changes in person-environment fit: A cross-level study. *Journal of Applied Psychology, 89*, 868–882.

Callen, J. L., Klein, A., & Tinkelman, D. (2003). Board composition, committees, and organizational efficiency: The case of nonprofits. *Nonprofit and Voluntary Sector Quarterly, 32*(4), 493–520.

Callen, J. L., Klein, A., & Tinkelman, D. (2009). The contextual impact of nonprofit board composition and structure on organizational performance: Agency and resource dependence perspectives. *Voluntas: International Journal of Voluntary and Nonprofit Organizations, 21*, 101–125.

Cameron, K. S., Bright, D., & Caza, A. (2004). Exploring the relationships between organizational virtuousness and performance. *American Behavioral Scientist, 47*(6), 766–790.

Cannella, B., Finkelstein, S., & Hambrick, D. C. (2008). *Strategic leadership: Theory and research on executives, top management teams, and boards*. Oxford University Press.

Cao, V. Q., & Ngo, T. T. T. (2019). Linking entrepreneurial intentions and mindset models: A comparative study of public and private universities in Vietnam. *Enterprise and Innovation Management Studies, 2*(2), 145–160.

Carman, J. G., & Nesbit, R. (2013). Founding new nonprofit organizations: Syndrome or symptom? *Nonprofit and Voluntary Sector Quarterly, 42*(3), 603–621.

Carroll, A. B. (2015). *Business and society: Ethics, sustainability, and stakeholder management*. Cengage Learning.

Chambliss, D. F., & Schutt, R. K. (2010). *Making sense of the social world: Methods of investigation*. Pine Forge Press.

Charmaz, K. (1983). The grounded theory method: An explication and interpretation. In R. M. Emerson (Ed.), *Contemporary field research* (pp. 109–126). Little, Brown.

Charmaz, K. (2000). Teachings of Anselm Strauss: Remembrances and reflections. *Sociological Perspectives., 43*(4), 163–174.

Charmaz, K. (2006). *Constructing grounded theory: Methods for the 21st century*. SAGE.

Charmaz, K. (2007). Reconstructing grounded theory. In L. Bickman, P. Alasuutari, & J. Brannen (Eds.), *Handbook of social research* (pp. 461–478). Sage.

Chell, E. (2007). Social enterprise and entrepreneurship: Towards a convergent theory of the entrepreneurial process. *International Small Business Journal, 25*(1), 5–26.

Chell, E. (2010). Social entrepreneurship and enterprise: International and innovation perspectives. *Entrepreneurship and Regional Development, 22*(6), 485–493.

Chelliah, A., & Panicker, A. S. (2016). Resilience and stress in children and adolescents with specific learning disability. *Journal of the Canadian Academy Child Adolescent Psychiatry, 25*(1), 17–23.

Chen, S. C., Chen, K. S., & Hsia, T. C. (2005). Promoting customer satisfactions by applying six sigma: An example from the automobile industry. *Quality Management Journal, 12*(4), 21–33.

Chirwa, D. M. (2016). *Combating child poverty: The role of economic, social and cultural rights*. Routledge.

Chirwa, E., & Dorward, A. (2011). The Malawi agricultural input subsidy program. *International Journal of Agricultural Sustainability, 9*(1), 232–247.

Christensen, L. B., Johnson, B., & Turner, L. A. (2014). *Research methods, design, and analysis*. Pearson.

Christensen, C. M., Mcdonald, R., Altman, E. J., & Palmer, J. E. (2018). Disruptive innovation: An intellectual history and directions for future research. *Journal of Management Studies, 55*(7), 1043–1078.

Christensen-Salem, A., Walumbwa, F. O., Babalola, M. T., Guo, L., & Misati, E. (2020). A multilevel analysis of the relationship between ethical leadership and ostracism: The roles of relational climate, employee mindfulness, and work unit structure. *Journal of Business Ethics*, 1–20. https://doi.org/10.1007/s10551-020-04424-5

Clarke, T. (1998). Research on corporate governance. *Corporate Governance. An International Review, 1*(6), 57–66.

Clausen, T. H., Korneliussen, T., & Madsen, E. L. (2013). Modes of innovation, resources and their influence on product innovation: Empirical evidence from R&D active firms in Norway. *Technovation, 33*(6–7), 225–233.

Coban, O., Ozdemir, S., & Pisapia, J. (2019). Top managers' organizational change management capacity and their strategic leadership levels at ministry of national education (MoNE). *Eurasian Journal of Educational Research, 19*(81), 1–18.
Cohen, B., & Warwick, M. (2006). *Values-driven business: How to change the world, make money, and have fun*. Berrett-Koehler Publishers.
Colebatch, H. K. (2017). *Policy*. Open University Press.
Cooper, C. (2015). Entrepreneurs of the self: the development of management control since 1976. Accounting, Organizations and Society, 47. pp. 14–24. ISSN 0361-3682, https://doi.org/10.1016/j.aos.2015.10.004
Cooper, J. M., & Strayer, D. L. (2015). Driven to distraction. *Human Factors, 57*(8), 1343–1347.
Corbin, J., & Strauss, A. (1990a). Grounded theory research: Procedures, canons and evaluative criteria. *Zeitschrift für Soziologie, 19*(6), 418–427.
Corbin, J. M., & Strauss, A. (1990b). Grounded theory research: Procedures, canons, and evaluative criteria. *Qualitative Sociology, 13*(1), 3–21.
Corbin, J., & Strauss, A. (2008). *Basics of qualitative research: Techniques and procedures for developing grounded theory*. Sage Publications.
Corbin, J. M., & Strauss, A. L. (2015). *Basics of qualitative research: Techniques and procedures for developing grounded theory*. Sage Publications.
Cornforth, C. (2001). *Power relations between boards and senior managers in the governance of public and nonprofit organizations*. Open University.
Cornforth, C., & Brown, W. A. (2013). *Nonprofit governance: Innovative perspectives and approaches*. Routledge.
Coupet, J., & Berrett, J. L. (2019). Toward a valid approach to nonprofit efficiency measurement. *Nonprofit Management and Leadership., 29*, 299–320. https://doi.org/10.1002/nml.21336
Crace, R. K., Hardy, C. J., & Crace, R. L. (2023). *Authentic excellence for organizations: Creating flourishing "&" cultures* (1st ed.). Routledge. https://doi.org/10.4324/9781003265726
Cravens, D. W., Piercy, N. F., & Baldauf, A. (2009). Management framework guiding strategic thinking in rapidly changing markets. *Journal of Marketing Management, 25*(2), 31–49.
Creswell, J. W. (2007). *Educational research: Planning, conducting, and evaluating quantitative and qualitative research*. Pearson.
Creswell, J. W. (2014). *Research design qualitative, quantitative, and mixed methods approaches*. Sage Publications.
Csikszentmihalyi, M. (2000). Happiness, flow, and economic equality. *American Psychologist, 55*(10), 1163–1164.
Csikszentmihalyi, M., & LeFevre, J. (1989). Optimal experience in work and leisure. *Journal of Personality and Social Psychology, 56*, 815–822.
Dart, R. (2004). The legitimacy of social enterprise. *Nonprofit Management and Leadership, 14*(4), 411–424.
Davis, R. C., & Mcclelland, D. C. (1962). The achieving society. *Technology and Culture, 3*(3), 351.
De Ruyter, K., Kleijnen, M., & Wetzels, M. (2007). An assessment of value creation in mobile service delivery and the moderating role of time consciousness. *Journal of Retailing, 83*(1), 33–46. ISSN 0022-4359.
de Vries, W. A. (1988). *Hegel's theory of mental activity*. Cornell University Press.
Deci, E. L., & Ryan, R. M. (2008). Hedonia, eudaimonia, and well-being: An introduction. *Journal of Happiness Studies, 9*, 1–11.
Dees, J. G. (2016). Social entrepreneurship. In M. Augier & D. J. Teece (Eds.), *The Palgrave encyclopedia of strategic management* (pp. 1–4). Palgrave Macmillan. https://doi.org/10.1057/978-1-349-94848-2_373-1
Dees, J. G., & Anderson, B. B. (2003). Sector-bending: Blurring lines between nonprofit and forprofit. *Society, 40*, 16–27.
Dees, J. G., Elias, J., & Bowie, N. E. (1998). The challenges of combining social and commercial enterprise. *Business Ethics Quarterly, 8*(1), 165–178.
Defourny, J., & Nyssens, M. (2006). *Social enterprise: At the crossroads of market, public policies and civil society*. Routledge.

Demir, K. (2015). The effect of organizational trust on the culture of teacher leadership in primary schools. *Educational Sciences: Theory & Practice, 15*(3), 621–634.
Den Hartog, D. N., House, R. J., Hanges, P. J., Ruiz-Quintanilla, S. A., Dorfman, P. W., Brenk, K. M., & Sabadin, A. (1999). Culture specific and cross culturally generalizable implicit leadership theories: Are attributes of charismatic/transformational leadership universally endorsed? *Leadership Quarterly, 10*(2), 219–252.
Denzin, N. K. (2010). Grounded and indigenous theories and the politics of pragmatism. *Sociological Inquiry, 80*, 296–312.
Denzin, N. K., & Lincoln, Y. S. (2005). *The SAGE handbook of qualitative research*. Sage Publications.
Dey, P. (2006). The rhetoric of social entrepreneurship: Paralogy and new language games in academic discourse. In C. Steyaert & D. Hjorth (Eds.), *Entrepreneurship as social change: A third movements in entrepreneurship book* (pp. 121–143). Edward Elgar.
Dey, P., & Teasdale, S. (2013). Social enterprise and dis/identification: The politics of identity work in the English third sector. *Administrative Theory and Praxis, 35*(2), 248–270.
Diener, E., & Diener, C. (2010). Monitoring psychosocial prosperity for social change. In R. Biswas-Diener (Ed.), *Positive psychology as social change* (pp. 53–71). Springer Science + Business Media.
Diener, E., Wirtz, D., Tov, W., Kim-Prieto, C., Choi, D., Oishi, S., & Biswas-Diener, R. (2010). New measures of well-being: Flourishing and positive and negative feelings. *Social Indicators Research, 39*, 247–266.
Dill, A. P., Zrinščak, S., & Coury, J. M. (2012). Nonprofit leadership development in the post-socialist context: The case of Croatia. *Administration in Social Work, 36*(3), 314–341.
Dinwoodie, D. (2014). *Leadership: Enhancing the lessons of experience*. McGraw-Hill Education.
Doherty, B., Haugh, H., & Lyon, F. (2014). *Social enterprises: An organizational perspective*. Palgrave Macmillan.
Doloreux, D., Shearmur, R., & Rodriguez, M. (2018). Internal R&D and external information in knowledge-intensive business service innovation: Complements, substitutes or independent? *Technological and Economic Development of Economy, 24*(6), 2255–2276.
Drayton, B. (2011). Collaborative entrepreneurship: How social entrepreneurs can tip the world by working in global teams. *Innovations: Technology, Governance, Globalization, 6*(2), 35–38.
Drayton, B. (2019). Everyone a changemaker--social entrepreneurship's ultimate goal: Creating a new civilization through social entrepreneurship, *MIT Press, 1*(1), 53–61.
Eikenberry, A. (2009). Refusing the market: A democratic discourse for voluntary and nonprofit organizations. *Nonprofit and Voluntary Sector Quarterly, 38*(4), 582–596.
Ekpenyong, D. B., & Umoren, N. J. (2010). Political risk and the business environment: An examination of core challenges. *Journal of Financial Management and Analysis, 23*(1), 27–32.
Fitzsimmons, J. A., & Bordoloi, S. (2014). *Service management: Operations, strategy, information technology* (10th ed.). McGraw-Hill Higher Education.
Fives, H., & DiDonato-Barnes, N. (2013). Classroom test construction: The power of a table of specifications. *Practical Assessment, Research, and Evaluation., 18*(1). https://doi.org/10.7275/cztt-7109
Fowers, B. J. (2012). An Aristotelian framework for the human good. *Journal of Theoretical and Philosophical Psychology, 32*(1), 10–23.
Fowers, B. J. (2015). *The evolution of ethics: Human sociality and the emergence of ethical mindedness*. Palgrave Macmillan.
Gatzert, N., Schmit, J. T., & Kolb, A. (2015). Assessing the risks of insuring reputation risk. *Journal of Risk and Insurance, 83*(3), 641–679.
Gawell, M. (2013). Social entrepreneurship: Action grounded in needs, opportunities and/or perceived necessities? *VOLUNTAS: International Journal of Voluntary and Nonprofit Organizations, 24*(4), 1071–1090.
Gelo, O., Braakmann, D., & Benetka, G. (2008). Quantitative and qualitative research: Beyond the debate. *Integrative Psychological & Behavioral Science, 42*(3), 266–290.
Gilkey, R. (2008). *Building a learning organization: A new role for human resource leaders*. JKL Publisher.

Glaser, B. G. (1992). *Basics of grounded theory analysis: Emergences vs forcing*. Sociology Press.
Glaser, B. G., & Strauss, A. L. (1967). *The discovery of grounded theory: Strategies for qualitative research*. Aldine de Gruyter.
Glaser, B. G., & Strauss, A. L. (1971). *Awareness of dying*. Routledge.
Glaser, B. G., & Strauss, A. L. (2009). *The discovery of grounded theory: Strategies for qualitative research*. Aldine.
Glendon, A. I., & Clarke, S. (2016). *Human safety and risk management: A psychological perspective* (3rd ed.). CRC Press. https://doi.org/10.1201/b19401
Gobble, M. M. (2016). Defining disruptive innovation. *Research-Technology Management, 59*(4), 66–71.
Gothard, S., & Austin, M. J. (2014). Leadership succession planning: Implications for nonprofit human service organizations. *Administration in Social Work, 37*(3), 272–285.
Graen, G. B., & Uhl-Bien, M. (1995). Relationship-based approach to leadership: Development of leader-member exchange (LMX) theory of leadership over 25 years: Applying a multi-level multi-domain perspective. *The Leadership Quarterly, 6*(2), 219–247.
Gray, J. (2006). *Intentionality and consciousness*. Stanford Encyclopedia of Philosophy.
Green, J. C., & Griesinger, D. W. (1996). Board performance and organizational effectiveness in nonprofit social services organizations. *Nonprofit Management and Leadership, 6*(4), 381–402.
Greenleaf, R. K. (1970). *The servant as leader*. Robert K. Greenleaf Center for Servant Leadership.
Greenleaf, R. K., & Spears, L. C. (2002). *Servant leadership: A journey into the nature of legitimate power and greatness*. Paulist Press.
Grenier, A. M., & Guberman, N. (2009). Creating and sustaining disadvantage: The relevance of a social exclusion framework. *Health & Social Care in the Community, 17*(2), 116–124.
Grossi, G., Reichard, C., Thomasson, A., & Vakkuri, J. (2017). Performance measurement of hybrid organizations. *Public Money & Management, 37*(6), 379–386.
Gürol, Y., & Atsan, N. (2006). Entrepreneurial characteristics amongst university students. *Education + Training, 48*(1), 25–38.
Haas, M., Munzer, B., Santen, S., Hopson, L., Haas, N., Overbeek, D., & Huang, R. (2019). Didactics revolution: Applying Kotter's 8-step change management model to residency didactics. *Western Journal of Emergency Medicine, 21*(1), 65–70.
Haeffele, S., & Storr, V. H. (2019). Understanding nonprofit social enterprises: Lessons from Austrian economics. *The Review of Austrian Economics*. https://doi.org/10.1007/s11138-019-00449-w
Hagen, E. E. (1967). *On the theory of social change: How economic growth begins*. The Dorsey Press.
Hall, D., & Hall, I. (1996). *Practical social research: Project work in the community*. Red Globe Press.
Hansmann, H. B. (1980). *The role of nonprofit enterprise*. Institution for Social and Policy Studies, Yale University.
Harding, R. (2010). *Hidden social enterprises: Why we need to look again at the numbers*. Delta/IFF Research.
Hartog, D. N., House, R. J., Hanges, P. J., Ruiz-Quintanilla, S. A., & Dorfman, P. W. (1999). Culture specific and cross-culturally generalizable implicit leadership theories: Are attributes of charismatic/transformational leadership universally endorsed? *The Leadership Quarterly, 10*, 219–256.
Harvard Business Review Press. (2011). *Harvard Business Review on thriving in emerging markets*. Harvard Business Review Press.
Harvey, D. (2017). *A brief history of neoliberalism*. Oxford University Press.
He, A. J., Shi, Y., & Liu, H. (2020). Crisis governance, Chinese style: Distinctive features of China's response to the Covid-19 pandemic. *Policy Design and Practice, 3*(3), 242–258. https://doi.org/10.1080/25741292.2020.1799911
Heaphy, E. D., & Dutton, J. E. (2008). Positive social interactions and the human body at work: Linking organizations and physiology. *Academy of Management Review, 33*(1), 137–162.
Heerad Sabeti, J., Meier, R., & Fisher, K. (2014). *The for-benefit enterprise*. Oxford University Press.

Helmsing, A. H. J. (2015). Conditions for social entrepreneurship. *International Journal of Social Quality., 5*, 51–66. https://doi.org/10.3167/IJSQ.2015.050104

Henton, D. C. (1997). *Grassroots leaders for a new economy: How civic entrepreneurs are building prosperous communities*. Jossey-Bass.

Higgin, G., & Finnie, P. (2010). *Organization and management in construction: Shaping theory and practice*. Wiley-Blackwell.

Hill, T. (2009). *Operations management*. Palgrave Macmillan.

Hisrich, R. D., Peters, M. P., & Shepherd, D. A. (2008). *Entrepreneurship*. McGraw-Hill.

Hitt, M. A., Ireland, R. D., & Hoskisson, R. E. (1998). *Strategic management: Competitiveness and globalization concepts and cases*. South-Western.

Hitt, M. A., Hoskisson, R. E., & Ireland, R. D. (2008). *Management of strategy: Concepts and cases*. South-Western Cengage Learning.

HM Treasury. (1999). *Enterprise and social exclusion*. HM Treasury National Strategy for Neighborhood Renewal Policy Action Team 3.

Homan, A. C., Gündemir, S., Buengeler, C., & Kleef, G. A. V. (2020). Leading diversity: Towards a theory of functional leadership in diverse teams. *Journal of Applied Psychology, 105*(10), 1101–1128.

Hood, C. (2006). A historical perspective on transparency. In C. Hood & D. A. Heald (Eds.), *Transparency: The key to better governance?* (pp. 3–23). British Academy/Oxford University Press.

Hopp, C., & Stephan, U. (2012). The influence of socio-cultural environments on the performance of nascent entrepreneurs: Community culture, motivation, self-efficacy and start-up success. *Entrepreneurship & Regional Development. An International Journal, 24*(9–10), 917–945.

Hornsby, J. S., Kuratko, D. F., Holt, D. T., & Wales, W. J. (2013). Assessing a measurement of organizational preparedness for corporate entrepreneurship. *Journal of Product Innovation Management, 30*(5), 937–955.

House, R. J., & Aditya, R. N. (1997). The social scientific study of leadership: Quo Vadis? *Journal of Management, 23*(3), 409–473.

Hung, C., & Wang, L. (2021). Institutional constraints, market competition, and revenue strategies: Evidence from Canadian social enterprises. *Voluntas: International Journal of Voluntary and Nonprofit Organizations*. https://doi.org/10.1007/s11266-020-00300-y

Hung, S.-Y., Ku, Y.-C., Liang, T.-P., & Lee, C.-C. (2019). *Social media in strategic management*. Emerald Publishing.

Huntsman, T., & Greer, S. (2019). *Strategic decision making: Applying the analytic hierarchy process*. Springer.

Hurka, T. (1999). The three faces of flourishing. *Social Philosophy and Policy, 16*(1), 44–71.

Hutchison, T., & Schumpeter, J. A. (1955). A history of economic analysis. *The Quarterly Journal of Economics, 69*(1), 1–22.

International Finance Corporation. (2014). *IFC annual report 2014: Growing solutions*. International Finance Corporation.

Ireland, R. D., Kuratko, D. F., & Morris, M. H. (2006). A health audit for corporate entrepreneurship: Innovation at all levels. *Journal of Business Strategy, 27*(1), 10–17.

Isenberg, M. A., & Woods, S. J. (2001). Adaptation as a mediator of intimate abuse and traumatic stress in battered women. *Nursing Science Quarterly, 14*(3), 215–221.

James, R., & Jones, R. (2013). Transferring the Toyota lean cultural paradigm into India: Implications for human resource management. *The International Journal of Human Resource Management, 25*(15), 2174–2191. https://doi.org/10.1080/09585192.2013.862290

Jaristrom, C., Andresen, T., & Hameed, F. (2018). *Global logistics and supply chain management*. Wiley.·

Jean-Baptiste, S. (2012). *On the market for entrepreneurs. Et Jean-Baptiste Say... Créa L'Entrepreneur*. Peter Lang.

Johnston, J. M., & Girth, A. M. (2012). Government contracts and "managing the market": Exploring the costs of strategic management responses to weak vendor competition. *Administration & Society, 44*(1), 3–29.

Jones, A. P., James, L. R., & Bruni, J. R. (1975). Perceived leadership behavior and employee confidence in the leader as moderated by job involvement. *Journal of Applied Psychology, 60*(1), 146–149.
Kadry, S., & Hami, A. E. (2018). *Innovations in e-systems for business and commerce*. Apple Academic Press.
Kahnerman, D., & Tversky, A. (1999). *Choices, values, and frames*. Cambridge University Press.
Kaluwa, M. (2015). Profitability and price flexibility in manufacturing of a developing country. *Journal of Industrial Economics, 39*(6), 689–700.
Kandoole, B., & Masten, J. (2000). The transfer of small business assistance strategies to emerging countries: The case of Malawi. *The Journal of Technology Transfer, 25*, 289–298.
Kanter, M., & Purrington, C. (1998). Lockheed Martin IMS: Making a contribution and a profit. *Harvard Business School Case Collections*, 399-018.
Kelly, P. (2009). *What technology wants*. Viking.
Keping, Y. (2018). *Governance and rule of law in China*. Brill.
Kerlin, J. A. (2006). Social enterprise in the United States and Europe: Understanding and learning from the differences. *International Journal of Voluntary and Nonprofit Organizations, 17*(3), 246–462.
Keyes, C. L. M. (2002). The mental health continuum: From languishing to flourishing in life. *Journal of Health and Social Research, 43*, 207–222.
Keyes, C. L. M. (2005). Mental illness and/or mental health? Investigating axioms of the complete state model of health. *Journal of Consulting and Clinical Psychology, 73*, 539–548.
Kieng, S., & Quack, S. (2012). *Governing corporate responsibility in the global economy: Markets, politics and institutions*. Edward Elgar Publishing.
Kim, W. C., & Mauborgne, R. (1999). Creating new market space: A systematic approach to value innovation can help companies break free from the competitive pack. *Harvard Business Review, 77*(1), 83–93.
Klenke, A. (2008). *Probability theory: Comprehensive course*. Springer.
Ko, W. W., & Liu, G. (2020). The transformation from traditional nonprofit organizations to social enterprises: An institutional entrepreneurship perspective. *Journal of Business Ethics*. https://doi.org/10.1007/s10551-020-04446-z
Koh, S. L., Demirbag, M., Bayraktar, E., Tatoglu, E., & Zaim, S. (2007). The impact of supply chain management practices on performance of SMEs. *Industrial Management & Data Systems, 107*(1), 103–124.
Korte, R. (2018). Identifying as an entrepreneur: A social identity perspective of the entrepreneurial mindset. *Advances in Engineering Education, 7*(1), 1–9.
Kotter, J. P. (1988). *The leadership factor*. Free Press.
Kotter, J. P. (2012). *Leading change*. Harvard Business Review Press.
Kram, K. E. (1985). *Mentoring at Work: Developmental Relationships in Organizational Life*. University Press of America.
Krug, K., & Weinberg, C. B. (2004). Mission, money, and merit: Strategic decision making by nonprofit managers. *Nonprofit Management and Leadership, 14*(3), 325–342.
Kumar, V., Barma, M., & Rajasekhar, S. S. N. (2020). Handling disruptive educational innovations: What determines the difference while embracing changes? *Medical Journal of Dr. D.Y. Patil Vidyapeeth, 13*(1), 8–10.
Kurtessis, J. N., Eisenberger, R., Ford, M. T., Buffardi, L. C., Stewart, K. A., & Adis, C. S. (2017). *Organizational support theory: The evolution of a theoretical construct*. Springer.
Lang, T. (2015). *Feeding Britain: Our food problems and how to fix them*. Pelican.
Laszlo, A., Laszlo, K., & Johnsen, C. (2012). *Fostering evolutionary leadership: Theory, ethics, and practice*. Emerald Group Publishing.
Leadbeater, C. (2006). The socially entrepreneurial city. In A. Nicholls (Ed.), *Social Entrepreneurship* (pp. 233–246). Oxford University Press.
Lee, J. W., Zhang, L., Dallas, M., & Chin, H. (2019). Managing relational conflict in Korean social enterprises: The role of participatory HRM practices, diversity climate, and perceived social impact. *Business Ethics: A European Review, 28*(1), 19–35.

Littlewood, J. (2018). *Public enterprises: Unresolved challenges and new opportunities*. OECD Publishing.
Littlewood, D., & Holt, D. (2015). Social entrepreneurship in South Africa: Exploring the influence of environment. *Business & Society, 57*(3), 525–561.
Littunen, H. (2000). Entrepreneurship and the characteristics of the entrepreneurial personality. *International Journal of Entrepreneurial Behavior & Research, 6*(6), 295–310.
Liu, Y., Fedor, D., Herold, D., & Caldwell, S. (2008). Leadership, organizational commitment, and change commitment: A multilevel investigation. *Journal of Organizational Change Management, 27*(6), 900–921.
Liu, F., He, Y., Zhang, A., Cui, J., Duan, P., & Xu, Y. (2018). Product assembling quality risk control strategy based on reverse RQR chain. *International Conference on Reliability, Maintainability, and Safety (ICRMS), 12*, 1–6.
Liu, Y., Cooper, C., & Tarba, S. (2019). Resilience, wellbeing and HRM: A multidisciplinary perspective. *The International Journal of Human Resource Management, 30*, 1227–1238. https://doi.org/10.1080/09585192.2019.1565370
Lopez, K. A., & Willis, D. G. (2004). Descriptive versus interpretive phenomenology: Their contributions to nursing knowledge. *Qualitative Health Research, 14*(5), 726–735.
López-Arceiz, F. J., Bellostas, A. J., & Rivera, P. (2023). Pilar are Mediterranean nonprofits adopting the social Enterprise model? *Voluntas: International Journal of Voluntary and Nonprofit Organizations*. https://doi.org/10.1007/s11266-023-00576-w
Luke, B., & Chu, V. (2013). Social enterprise versus social entrepreneurship: An examination of the "why" and "how" in pursuing social change. *International Small Business Journal, 31*(7), 764–784.
Macedonian Business Monthly. (2015). Macedonian companies interested in innovations. *Macedonian Business Monthly, 16*(161), 2–9.
MacIntyre, A. (2002). *Dependent rational animals: Why human beings need the virtues*. Open Court.
MacIntyre, A. (2007). *After virtue: A study in moral theory* (3rd ed.). University of Notre Dame Press.
MacIntyre, A. (2015). The irrelevance of ethics. In A. Bielskis & K. Knight (Eds.), *Virtue and economy: Essays on morality and markets* (pp. 7–21). Ashgate.
MacIntyre, P. D., & Mercer, S. (2014). Introducing positive psychology to SLA. *Studies in Second Language Learning and Teaching, 4*(2), 153–172.
Maclean, M., Harvey, C., & Chia, R. (2012). Sensemaking, storytelling and the legitimization of elite business careers. *Human Relations, 65*(1), 17–40.
Maddalena, V. (2012). A primer on project management. *Leadership in Health Services, 25*(2), 80–89.
Mahmood, I., Chung, C.-N., & Mitchell, W. (2017). Political connections and business strategy in dynamic environments: How types and destinations of political ties affect business diversification in closed and open political economic contexts. *Global Strategy Journal, 7*(4), 375–399.
Manders, A., Myers, J. K., & Smith, L. A. (2020). *Creating a data-driven organization: Practical advice from the trenches*. O'Reilly Media.
Mathisen, G., Øgaard, T., & Marnburg, E. (2013). Women in the boardroom: How do female directors of corporate boards perceive boardroom dynamics? *Journal of Business Ethics, 116*. https://doi.org/10.1007/s10551-012-1461-9
Maxwell, J. A. (2013). *Qualitative research design: An interactive approach*. SAGE Publications.
Mayo, E. (2017). *The ecology of commerce: A declaration of sustainability*. Harper Business.
Mcclelland, D. C. (1961). *The achieving society*. Van Nostrand.
McLellan, R., & Steward, S. (2015). Measuring children and young people's wellbeing in the school context. *Cambridge Journal of Education, 45*, 307–332.
Medlin, C. J., & Ellegaard, C. (2015). Conceptualizing competition and rivalry in a networking business market. *Industrial Marketing Management, 51*, 131–140.
Ménard, C. (2004). The economics of hybrid organizations. *Journal of Institutional and Theoretical Economics (JITE) /Zeitschrift Für Die Gesamte Staatswissenschaft, 160*(3), 345–376. http://www.jstor.org/stable/40752467

Mikołajczak, P. (2020). Social enterprises' hybridity in the concept of institutional logics: Evidence from Polish NGOs. *VOLUNTAS: International Journal of Voluntary and Nonprofit Organizations*. https://doi.org/10.1007/s11266-020-00195-9
Miles, M., & Huberman, A. M. (1994). *Qualitative data analysis: An expanded sourcebook*. Sage Publications.
Miles, M. B., Huberman, A. M., & Saldaña, J. (2013). *Qualitative data analysis: A methods sourcebook*. Sage Publications.
Mintzberg, H. (1978). Patterns in strategy formation. *Management Science, 24*(9), 934–948.
Mintzberg, H. (2003). *The strategic management: Concepts and contexts*. Prentice Hall.
Moghalu, K. C. (2014). *Emerging Africa: How the global economy's last frontier can prosper and matter*. Penguin Publications.
Morand, D. A., & Merriman, K. K. (2012). "Equality theory" as a counterbalance to equity theory in human resource management. *Journal of Business Ethics, 111*, 133–144. https://doi.org/10.1007/s10551-012-1435-y
Moulaert, F., & Ailenei, O. (2005). Social economy, third sector and solidarity relations: A conceptual synthesis from history to present. *Urban Studies, 42*(11), 2037–2053.
MSME Policy. (2012). *Micro, small, and medium enterprises policy framework*. Government of India Publications.
Myers, D. G. (2000). The funds, friends, and faith of happy people. *American Psychologist, 55*(1), 56–67.
Neveu, J.-P., & Kakavand, B. (2019). Endangered resources: The role of organizational justice and interpersonal trust as signals for workplace corruption. *Relations Industrielles, 74*(3), 498–524.
Ng, A. K., Ho, D. Y. F., Wong, S. S., & Smith, I. (2003). In search of the good life: A cultural odyssey in the East and West. *Genetic, Social, and General Psychology Monographs, 129*, 317–363.
Ngomane, R. M., & Mahlangu, E. (2014). Leadership mentoring and succession in the Charismatic churches in Bushbuckridge. *HTS Teologiese Studies/Theological Studies, 70*(1), 1–10.
Ngwira, K. (2016). *The road to entrepreneurship a sure way to become wealth at individual, business and state levels*. Author House.
Ngwira, A., Thierfelder, C., & Lambert, D. (2014). Conservation agriculture systems for Malawian smallholder farmers: Long-term effects on crop productivity, profitability and soil quality. *Renewable Agriculture and Food Systems, 28*(4), 350–363.
Nicholls, A. (2010). Institutionalizing social entrepreneurship in regulatory space: Reporting and disclosure by community interest companies. *Accounting, Organizations and Society, 35*(4), 394–415.
Northouse, P. G. (2013). *Leadership*. SAGE.
O'Reilly, C., & Binns, A. J. M. (2019). The three stages of disruptive innovation: Idea generation, incubation, and scaling. *California Management Review, 61*(3), 49–71.
Olson, D. L., & Wu, D. D. (2010). *Enterprise risk management*. World Scientific Publication.
Osberg, S. R., & Martin, R. L. (2015). Two keys to sustainable social enterprise economics & society. *Harvard Business Review, 5*, 86–94.
Oster, S. M. (1995). *Strategic management for nonprofit organizations: Theory and cases*. Oxford University Press.
Owusu-Ansah, J. P. (2004). *Making the visible invisible: The impact of extension agent attitudes towards farmers on extension projects and policy: The case of Uganda*. J.P. Owusu-Ansah.
Ozyilmaz, A., Erdogan, B., & Karaeminogullari, A. (2019). Trust in organization as a moderator of the relationship between self-efficacy and workplace outcomes: A social cognitive theory-based examination. *Journal of Occupational and Organizational Psychology, 91*(1), 181–204.
Page, L., Boysen, S., & Arya, T. (2019). Creating a culture that thrives: Fostering respect, trust, and psychological safety in the workplace. *OD Practitioner, 51*(1), 28–35.
Parker, P. (2019). *Remote Work Revolution: Succeeding from Anywhere*. Harper Business.
Parker, L. D., & Roffey, B. H. (1997). Methodological themes. *Accounting, Auditing & Accountability Journal, 10*(2), 212–247.
Patton, P. (2001). Postmodernism: Philosophical aspects. In N. J. Smelser & P. B. Baltes (Eds.), *International encyclopedia of the social & behavioral sciences* (pp. 11872–11877). Pergamon.

Peter, T., Sendawula, K., Pedson, T., & Saadat, N. K. (2019). The joint effect of firm capability and access to finance on firm performance among small businesses: A developing country perspective. *African Journal of Business Management, 13*(6), 198–206. https://doi.org/10.5897/AJBM2019.8758

Pizarro, E. F., González, M., & Javier, F. (2022). Creation of work integration social enterprises (WISEs) by social action organizations: Proposal of a model for decision-making. *Voluntas: International Journal of Voluntary and Nonprofit Organizations.* https://doi.org/10.1007/s11266-021-00447-2

Porter, M. E. (1979). How competitive forces shape strategy. *Harvard Business Review, 57*(2), 137–145.

Porter, M. E. (1980). *Competitive strategy techniques for analyzing industries and competitors.* Free Press.

Porter, M. E. (1985). *Competitive Advantage: Creating and Sustaining Superior Performance.* Free Press.

Porter, M.E. (2008). The five competitive forces that shape strategy. *Harvard Business Review.*

Porter, M. E., & Kramer, M. R. (2006). Strategy and society: The link between competitive advantage and corporate social responsibility. *National Library of Medicine, 84*(12), 78–92.

Powell, W. W., & Steinberg, R. (2006). *The nonprofit sector: A research handbook.* Yale University Press.

Praszkier, R., & Nowak, R. (2011). *Social entrepreneurship: Theory and concept.* Cambridge University Press.

Purdy, J. M., & Lawless, J. (2011). Building a culture of integrity. In C. Wankel & A. Stachowicz-Stanusch (Eds.), *Handbook of research in teaching ethics in business and management education* (pp. 427–440). Information Science Reference.

Purdy, J. M., & Lawless, J. (2012). Learning about governance through nonprofit board service. *Journal of Management Education, 36*(1), 33–65.

Raelin, J. A. (2011). *Creating leaderful organizations: How to bring out leadership in everyone.* ReadHowYouWant.

Raelin, J. A. (2014). Imagine there are no leaders: Reframing leadership as collaborative agency. *Leadership, 12*(2), 77–99.

Rasmussen, E., Mosey, S., & Wright, M. (2011). The evolution of entrepreneurial competencies: A longitudinal study of university spin-off venture emergence. *Journal of Management Studies, 48*, 1314–1345. https://doi.org/10.1111/j.1467-6486.2010.00995.x

Rask, K., Harris, A., & Thompson, L. (2020). *Financial literacy and investment decisions.* McGraw-Hill.

Rawhouser, H., Cummings, M., & Newbert, S. L. (2019). Social impact measurement: Current approaches and future directions for social entrepreneurship research. *Entrepreneurship Theory and Practice, 43*(1), 82–115.

Rentes, V. C., Pádua, S. I. D. D., Coelho, E. B., Ilana, G. G. F., & Rozenfeld, H. (2019). Implementation of a strategic planning process oriented towards promoting business process management (BPM) at a Clinical Research Center (CRC). *Business Process Management Journal, 25*(4), 707–737.

Rothmann, S. (2017). Employee engagement. In L. G. Oades, M. Steger, A. Delle-Fave, & J. Passmore (Eds.), *The Wiley-Blackwell handbook of the psychology of positivity and strengths-based approaches at work* (pp. 317–341). Wiley.

Rothmann, S., & Welsh, C. (2013). Employee engagement: The role of psychological conditions. *Management Dynamics: Journal of the Southern African Institute for Management Scientists, 22*(1), 14–25.

Ruttan, V. W. (1997). Induced innovation, evolutionary theory and path dependence: Sources of technical change. *The Economic Journal, 107*(444), 1520–1529.

Ryan, R. M., & Deci, E. L. (2001). On happiness and human potentials: A review of research on Hedonic and Eudaimonic well-being. *Annual Review of Psychology, 52*, 141–166.

Sabeti, H., Jones, M., & Clark, L. (2014). *Innovative approaches to funding social enterprises.* Routledge.

Salamzadeh, A., & Kesim, H. K. (2015). Startup companies: Life cycle and challenges. *Entrepreneurship & Management e-Journal*. https://doi.org/10.2139/ssrn.2628861
Salamzadeh, A., Salamzadeh, Y., & Nejati, M. (2012). Social entrepreneurship: Analyzing literature and proposing a comprehensive model. In *Proceedings of the 9th Asian Academy of Management international conference* (Vol. 14, pp. 520–525).
Saldaña, J., Saldaña, J., & Miles, M. B. (2013). *The coding manual for qualitative researchers + qualitative data analysis: A methods sourcebook*. Sage Publications.
Salicru, S. (2014). *Leadership results: How to create adaptive leaders and high-performing organisations for an uncertain world*. Wiley.
Salmon, P. (2008). *Emotional intelligence in everyday life*. Psychology Press.
Scharmer, O., & Käufer, K. (2013). *Leading from the emerging future from ego-system to eco-system economies*. Berrett-Koehler.
Schneider, B., González-Romá, V., Ostroff, C., & West, M. A. (2017). Organizational climate and culture: Reflections on the history of the constructs. *Journal of Applied Psychology, 102*(3), 468–482.
Schöning, M., & Noble, A. (2012). *The governance of social enterprises managing your organization for success*. Schwab Foundation for Social Entrepreneurship. https://doi.org/10.2139/ssrn.2018937
Schotanus-Dijkstra, M. (2016). *Positieve Psychologie: Wetenschap van Geluk en Welzijn*. Springer.
Schumpeter, J. A. (1934). *The theory of economic development*. Harvard University Press.
Schumpeter, J. (1949). Economic theory and entrepreneurial history. In R. R. Wohl (Ed.), *Change and the Entrepreneur: Postulates and the Patterns for Entrepreneurial History* (pp. 131–142). Harvard University Press.
Sears, G., & Ng, E. S. (2011). CEO leadership and the implementation of organizational diversity practices. *Journal of Business Ethics, 105*(1), 41–52.
Seligman, M. E. P. (2010). *Learned optimism: How to change your mind and your life*. Vintage.
Seligman, M. E. P. (2011). *Flourish: A visionary new understanding of happiness and well-being*. Atria Books.
Seligman, M. E., & Csikszentmihalyi, M. (2000). Positive psychology: An introduction. *American Psychologist, 55*(1), 5–14.
Seligman, M. E. P., & Pawelski, J. O. (2003). Positive psychology FAQs. *Psychological Inquiry, 14*(2), 159–163.
Sendjaya, S., & Sarros, J. C. (2002). Servant leadership: Its origin, development, and application in organizations. *Journal of Leadership & Organizational Studies, 6*(1/2), 49–72.
Senge, P. M. (2005). Missing the boat on leadership. *Leader to Leader, 38*(1), 20–30.
Sepulveda, L. (2012). Social enterprise and ethnic minorities: Exploring the consequences of the evolving British policy agenda. *Environment and Planning C: Government and Policy, 31*(4), 633–648.
Shanock, L. R., Baran, B. E., Gentry, W. A., Pattison, S. C., & Heggestad, E. D. (2019). Polynomial regression with response surface analysis: A practical guide for career management researchers. *Journal of Career Development, 46*(1), 10–24.
Shen, J., & Zhang, H. (2019). Socially responsible human resource management and employee support for external CSR: Roles of organizational CSR climate and perceived CSR directed toward employees. *Journal of Business Ethics, 156*(3), 875–888.
Shier, M., Handy, F., & Jennings, C. (2019). Intraorganizational conditions supporting social innovations by human service nonprofits. *Nonprofit and Voluntary Sector Quarterly, 48*(1), 173–193.
Shivji, I. G. (2007). *Silences in NGO discourse: The role and future of NGOs in Africa*. Fahamu.
Sirkkunen, E., & Cook, C. (2013). What's in a niche? Exploring the business model of online journalism. *Journal of Media Business Studies, 10*(4), 63–82.
Smilor, R. W. (1987). Commercializing technology through new business incubators. *Research Management, 30*(5), 36–41.
Smilor, R. (1997). Entrepreneurship: Reflections on a subversive activity. *Journal of Business Venturing, 12*(5), 341–346.

Smith, J. A., Flowers, P., & Larkin, M. H. (2013). *Interpretative phenomenological analysis: Theory, method and research*. Sage Publication.

Spear, R. (2001). A wide range of social enterprises. In C. Borzaga & J. Defourny (Eds.), *The emergence of social enterprise* (pp. 350–370). Routledge.

Stern, P. N., & Porr, C. J. (2011). *Essentials of accessible grounded theory*. Left Coast Press.

Stone, M. M., & Ostrower, F. (2007). Acting in the public interest? Another look at research on nonprofit governance. *Nonprofit and Voluntary Sector Quarterly, 20*(3), 429–443.

Strauss, A. L. (1998). *Qualitative analysis in social research: Grounded theory methodology*. SAGE.

Suddaby, R. (2006). From the editors: What grounded theory is not. *Academy of Management Journal, 49*, 633–642.

Sushandoyo, D., & Magnusson, T. (2014). Strategic niche management from a business perspective: Taking cleaner vehicle technologies from prototype to series production. *Journal of Cleaner Production, 74*, 17–26.

Suykens, B., George, B., De Rynck, F., & Verschuere, B. (2021). Determinants of non-profit commercialism. Resource deficits, institutional pressures or organizational contingencies? *Public Management Review, 23*(10), 1456–1478. https://doi.org/10.1080/14719037.2020.1764083

Svensson, G., et al. (2020). *Sustainable Development and Corporate Social Responsibility*. Springer.

Svensson, G., Wood, G., & Callaghan, M. (2020a). *Corporate responsibility and sustainable development: Exploring the Nexus of private and public interests*. Routledge.

Svensson, G., Wood, G., & Callaghan, M. (2020b). *Business ethics: Through time and across contexts*. Wiley.

Tahmasebifard, H. (2018). The role of competitive intelligence and its sub-types on achieving market performance. *Cogent Business & Management, 5*(1), 1–16.

Tan, W. L., Williams, J. N., & Tan, T. M. (2005). Defining the social in social entrepreneurship: Altruism and entrepreneurship. *International Entrepreneurship and Management Journal, 1*(3), 353–365.

Teasdale, S. (2010). *What's in a name? Making sense of social enterprise discourses*. Routledge.

Thau, S., Bennett, R. J., Mitchell, M. S., & Marrs, M. B. (2007). How management style moderates the relationship between abusive supervision and workplace deviance: A four-sample study. *Journal of Applied Psychology, 92*(4), 1123–1134.

Titchen, A., & Niessen, T. (2011). Living research practices. In J. Higgs, A. Titchen, D. Horsfall, & D. Bridges (Eds.), *Creative spaces for qualitative research, practice, education, work and society* (pp. 147–158). Sense Publishers.

Torsak, S., Piangkhae, P., Sunan, S., & Prayoon, C. (2019). Strategic leadership factors of school administrators influencing the effectiveness of small-sized schools. *International Journal of Educational Administration and Policy Studies, 11*(3), 20–28.

Trebesch, S. G. (2015). *Made to flourish beyond quick fixes to a thriving organization*. IVP Books.

Tuber, S. (2019). *Attachment, Play, and Authenticity: A Winnicott Primer*. Rowman & Littlefield.

Tucker, B. P., & Parker, L. D. (2013). Out of control? Strategy in the NFP sector: The implications for management control. *Accounting, Auditing & Accountability Journal, 26*(2), 234–266.

Turpin, A., & Shier, M. L. (2023). Social entrepreneurial orientation in nonprofits: The development and testing of a multidimensional scale. *VOLUNTAS: International Journal of Voluntary and Nonprofit Organizations*. https://doi.org/10.1007/s11266-023-00583-x

Varela, R., & Jimenez, J. E. (2001). The effect of entrepreneurship education in the universities of Cali. In W. D. William (Ed.), *Frontiers of entrepreneurship research. Proceedings of 21 annual Babson College entrepreneurship research conference* (pp. 543–587). Kauffman Foundation.

Vedenik, G., & Leber, M. (2015). Change management with the aid of a generic model for restructuring business processes. *International Journal of Simulation Modelling, 14*(4), 584–595.

Venkataraman, S. (1997). The distinctive domain of entrepreneurship research. In *Advances in entrepreneurship, firm emergence and growth* (Vol. 3, pp. 119–138). JAI Press.

Vesper, K. H. (1980). New venture planning. *Journal of Business Strategy, 1*(2), 73–75.

Walker, A., Hallinger, P., & Bajunid, I. (2002). *Leadership development in Asia-Pacific: Comparative perspectives*. Swets & Zeitlinger.

Walsh, I., Holton, J. A., Bailyn, L., Fernandez, W., Levina, N., & Glaser, B. (2015). What grounded theory is…a critically reflective conversation among scholars. *Organizational Research Methods, 18*(4), 589–599.

Waterman, A. S. (1993). Two conceptions of happiness: Contrasts of personal expressiveness (eudaimonia) and hedonic enjoyment. *Journal of Personality and Social Psychology, 64*, 678–691.

Weisbrod, B. A. (1998). Guest editor's introduction: The nonprofit mission and its financing. *Journal of Policy Analysis and Management, 17*(2), 165–174.

Wertz, F. J., Charmaz, K., McMullen, L. M., Josselson, R., Anderson, R., & McSpadden, E. (2011). *Five ways of doing qualitative analysis: Phenomenological psychology, grounded theory, discourse analysis, narrative research, and intuitive inquiry*. The Guilford Press.

Wheeler, L., & Reis, H. T. (1991). Self-recording of everyday life events. *Journal of Personality, 59*, 339–354.

Will, T. (2016). Flock leadership: Understanding and influencing emergent collective behavior. *The Leadership Quarterly, 27*(2), 261–279.

Williamson, O. E., Wachter, M. L., & Harris, J. E. (2011). *Transaction cost economics: The governance of contractual relations*. Cambridge University Press.

Winnard, J., Adcroft, A., Lee, J., & Skipp, D. (2014). Surviving or flourishing? Integrating business resilience and sustainability. *Journal of Strategy and Management, 7*(3), 303–315.

Winnard, J., Lee, J., & Skipp, D. (2017). Putting resilient sustainability into strategy decisions case studies. *Management Decision, 56*(7), 598–1612.

World Bank. (2012). *Governance matters 2012: Worldwide governance indicators, 1996–2008. Country data reports*. http://info.worldbank.org/governance/wgi/pdf/WBI_GovInd.pdf

World Bank. (2017). *World development report 2017: Governance and the law*. World Bank Publications.

World Bank. (2018a). *Poverty & equity data portal*. The World Bank Group.

World Bank. (2018b). *Malawi economic monitor: Investing in girls' education*. World Bank. https://openknowledge.worldbank.org/handle/10986/30902

Wright, J., Creighton, J., & Thiele, J. (2012). *Leadership in action: Effective strategies and tools*. Harvard Business Review Press.

Yang Y., & Konrad, A. M. (2011). Understanding diversity management practices: Implications of institutional theory and resource-based theory. *Group & Organization Management, 36*(1), 6–38.

Yukl, G. A. (2008). *Leadership in organizations*. Prentice Hall.

Yukl, G. A. (2010). *Ethical leadership questionnaire*. Prentice Hall.

Youssef-Morgan, C., & Luthans, F. (2007). Positive psychological capital: Beyond human and social capital. *Business Horizons, 47*(1), 45–50.

Yusuf, J.-E., & Sloan, M. F. (2015). Effectual processes in nonprofit start-ups and social entrepreneurship: An illustrated discussion of a novel decision-making approach. *The American Review of Public Administration, 45*(4), 417–435.

Zalta, E. N. (Ed.). (2004). *The Stanford encyclopedia of philosophy*. The Metaphysics Research Lab.

Printed in the USA
CPSIA information can be obtained
at www.ICGtesting.com
CBHW071519040824
12687CB00003B/121

9 783031 602337